Rites & Ceremonies

A PRACTICAL GUIDE

TO ALTERNATIVE

Funerals

KATE GORDON

CONSTABLE · LONDON

First published in Great Britain 1999 by Constable & Company Limited
3 The Lanchesters, 162 Fulham Palace Road, London W6 9ER
Copyright © Kate Gordon 1999
The right of Kate Gordon to be identified as author of this work has been
asserted by her in accordance with the Copyright,
Designs and Patents Act 1988
ISBN 0 09 478770 0
Set in Monotype Imprint by Rowland Phototypesetting Ltd
Printed in Great Britain by St Edmundsbury Press Ltd
both of Bury St Edmunds, Suffolk

A CIP catalogue record for this book is available from the British Library

CONTENTS

CONTENTS

CONTENTS

ACKNOWLEDGEMENTS

The following people have given me a great deal of advice and support in the compilation of this book and I am extremely grateful for their time and effort, so willingly given: Rev. Canon Colin Hill (Church of England); Rev. Peter Bell (CONCORD, Leeds); Annie Wildwood (Dragonpaths); Haviland Nye (British Buddhist Association); Robert Asby (executive director of the British Humanist Association); Anne Hosking (at the Religious Society of Friends); Marlena Schmool (Board of Deputies of British Jews); John Clifford (General Assembly of Unitarian and Free Christian Churches); Rev. Peter Norton, Ken West, Rev. John Clifford (General Assembly of Unitarian and Free Christian Churches); Sheila Page; the staff of Penrith Library who obtained a lot of my research material; my agent Richard Gollner for his sensible advice; my editor Carol O'Brien and the staff at Constable Publishers; and all the people who talked to me and shared their experiences so freely but who did not want to be identified in print.

Thanks also to Macmillan General Books for permission to quote from *The Collected Poems and Plays* of Rabindranath Tagore; the British Humanist Association for permission to quote from *Funerals without God*; Philip Carr-Gomm for permission to quote from his book *The Druid Way*; Clare Crossman for permission to include *End Page*; the Society of Authors and Mrs Nicolette Gray for permission to include *The Burning of Leaves* by Laurence Binyon; Virago Press for *Tropical Death* by Grace Nichols and 'Death is a clean bold word' by Rebecca Richmond; Seren Books and Mrs Gwynneth Lewis for *Postscript: For Gweno* by Alun Lewis; Penguin for extracts from *The Cloud of Unknowing*; Bloodaxe Press for *Belief* by Ann Thorp, *Found Lines* by Pamela Gillilan and *Prayer for the Little Daughter between Death and Burial* by Diana Scott; the estate of Dylan Thomas for 'And death shall have no dominion' and 'Do not go gentle into that good night'; Random House for *Oh Earth, Wait for Me* by Pablo Neruda; Oxford University Press for *On the Death of a Child* by D. J. Enright; Chatto and Windus for *Not to be Born* by David Sutton; Carcanet Press for *A Child Born Dead* by Elizabeth Jennings; the estate of Sylvia Plath for *Last Words*;

Academy Chicago for *Farewell Sweet Dust* by Elinor Wylie; A. M. Heath and Co. for *Dirge without Music* by Edna St Vincent Millay; Hodder Headline plc for permission to quote from Leslie Weatherhead's *A Private House of Prayer*; Hamish Hamilton for permission to reproduce from *Scala coeli* and *The Hollow Hill* by Kathleen Raine; Faber and Faber for 'Stop all the clocks' by W. H. Auden; extracts from *The Prophet* by Kahlil Gibran are used by permission of the National Committee of Gibran, all rights reserved; the Central Board of Finance of the Church of England for permission to quote from the liturgy; extracts from the Book of Common Prayer, the rights in which are vested in the Crown, are reproduced by permission of the Crown's Patentee, Cambridge University Press. Every effort has been made by the author to trace copyright holders. The author and publishers would be pleased to hear from anyone whose name has been omitted due to incorrect information.

INTRODUCTION

Death belongs to life as birth does
Rabindranath Tagore, *Stray Birds*

The seventeenth-century philosopher Francis Bacon
wrote that 'Men fear death as children fear to go in
the dark'. In the twentieth century fear and death
still go hand in hand for many people. If we have
no religious beliefs, we are afraid of nothingness (as
Bacon put it, 'to be we know not what, we know not
where'), or, if we are religious, the fear may be of
failure to attain the blissful afterlife and thus to spend
an eternity in 'outer darkness'. Death is a mystery,
a threshold, a final destination, the only certainty of
our lives, but ironically the one event we do not
like to contemplate in advance. This unwillingness
is reflected in the euphemisms we use to avoid talking
about it – 'passing away', 'crossing over', 'falling
asleep', or more brutally colloquial, 'kicking the

bucket', 'popping your clogs'. Our feelings about death surface in oblique ways. When we grieve for others, we are also grieving for our own mortality.

Death often comes unexpectedly, with little time to prepare for what is one of the most traumatic events of our lives – the funeral of a close friend or relative. It is also something for which we have little practice. You find yourself, within the space of a few days, having to cope with a complex legal situation and the arrangements for a funeral at a time when you are likely to be in a highly emotional state. Most people, without realising that there are other choices, take the easiest and most expensive option – the employment of a funeral director who will arrange everything for them.

There is a widespread belief that having a professional funeral director is a legal necessity. But, as the cost of a funeral rises, there is a growing number of people who are no longer able to afford their services. The DHSS funeral grant is paid only if everyone in the immediate family is entitled to benefits and it is wholly inadequate to cover the costs of the average funeral, which currently stands at around £1000. But it is not necessary to have a professional firm of undertakers and a DIY ceremony costs only a fraction of their fee. There are also several firms willing to do a 'part funeral', or assist people to organise their own (see address list below). This is obviously much cheaper.

Sixty years ago most people died at home. They

were laid out by a friend or neighbour – sometimes the local midwife – and their body was kept at home, either in the spare bedroom or on trestles in the parlour. Friends and family came to pay their respects, a local joiner made the coffin (plain or fancy depending on their means), the vicar, priest or minister was asked to conduct the funeral service and the sexton was paid to dig a grave in the local cemetery. If the family could afford it, they hired a hearse to take the coffin to the church; if they could not, it went on the back of a horse and cart, often lent by a local trader, draped in black and decorated especially for the day. In very poor areas, the body was pushed to church on a handcart, wrapped in a shroud.

At all stages the family and the community were fully involved in the process of bereavement, and the expense was minimal. Since the 1950s there has been an increasing trend to take death away from families and 'professionalise' it. This has not only led to escalating costs as the funeral business becomes a commercial industry, but the depersonalisation of the process makes it more difficult for the bereaved to come to terms with death and has led to a growing demand for bereavement counselling and the prescription of anti-depressants and tranquillisers.

Dr Elisabeth Kübler-Ross, one of the world's leading experts on dealing with death, in her book *On Death and Dying* tells the story of a relative who was terminally ill. 'When he did die, he was left in his own home, which he had built, and among his friends and neighbors who went to take a last look at him where he lay in the midst of flowers in the place he had lived in and loved so. In that country today there is still no make-believe slumber room, no embalming, no false make-up to pretend sleep.' Such a state of 'natural death', writes Dr Kübler-Ross, 'helps the dying patient as well as his family to accept the loss of a loved one'.

During the last fifty years there have been many changes in the way we deal with death. The limited number and increasing expense of burial sites has led to the growth of cremation as most people's choice of 'last rite'. The short time slot allowed at crematoria (only twenty minutes in some areas), the impersonal service taken by someone who never knew the deceased, and the feeling of being on a conveyor belt between one service and another, has led to growing dissatisfaction with the system. Relatives and friends often leave the crematorium bewildered, feeling that the ceremony failed both themselves and the deceased. While the best practice provides a caring and uplifting experience, many fall short of the ideal. A BBC radio documentary entitled *Undertaken with Love*, describing Jane Spottiswoode's attempts to arrange a funeral for her husband, inspired numerous letters from grieving relatives. One man told the horrific story of a chaplain who called his mother by the wrong name throughout the service. Another said that 'the actions of the ministers and the attitudes of funeral directors only added further grief and distress to the proceedings.'

A funeral service should be the celebration of a life and provide a secure environment for the expression of grief. In the words of Joseph Campbell, a funeral also allows us to 'meditate on death and the mystery of death'. Friends and family should come away comforted, feeling that the ceremony 'did justice' to the person they loved and knew.

Several cultures celebrate funerals with colourful processions, decorated coffins, music, singing and dancing – there are many ideas that could be incorporated into traditional Western rituals to enrich them. The idea of a 'green' funeral is gaining in popularity – you can opt to be buried in a green-field site in a biodegradable container and have a tree planted beside you. A memorial plaque will make it possible for relatives to visit the site of your grave in what will, in time, become beautiful natural woodland. Alternatively, you could be buried in your own back garden!

With the increasing popularity of cremation – something of a necessity as land for burial becomes more difficult to obtain – it has become necessary to have some kind of ceremonial for the scattering of ashes. Many people invent their own, reading a favourite piece of poetry or prose and saying goodbye in their own way. Others feel self-conscious and would welcome a ceremony that they could use.

Remembering the dead is very important. It's a

link with our own past, providing a sense of continuity for the living. It is also a way of giving them immortality. One of the traditional ways to remember the dead was to provide a lasting memorial – a tumulus, pyramid, carved tomb, a statue or public monument, carved head stone or a plaque. Some of these options are still open to us. A carved stone in a cemetery (though there are restrictions on size, shape, form and inscription) or a plaque are the most affordable. In European countries, gravestones often include photographs or portraits of the deceased set into the stone behind glass. For public figures or for anyone with sufficient means, a larger monument or commissioned artwork in an appropriate public place may be possible. But there are other ways. Plant a tree – something slow-growing like oak or yew (yew trees last for hundreds of years). Buy a birdbath or sundial for the garden and have it engraved to commemorate the deceased. Write a memorial page for the Virtual Garden of Remembrance on the Internet. Commission a seat for a public garden or buy a bed for the local hospital. Above all, keep your own record of a loved one's life, including a book of condolences with photographs of the funeral, special readings, letters and cards received; ask everyone who was there to sign the book, if possible also encouraging them to write a small message, or some particular memory.

It is often a good idea to hold a memorial service a few months after the death, or perhaps on the first anniversary – particularly if the deceased was a prominent figure in the community, or a member of an association or club with a lot of friends and associates. The family may want to have a small private funeral ceremony and a more public memorial service later.

COPING WITH GRIEF

One of the most ancient and fundamental functions of the funeral ceremony is to help friends and relatives to work through their grief and come to terms with the loss of someone they loved. The death of someone close is one of the most traumatic events we ever have to cope with. Whatever emotions we have about that person – love, dislike or a more complicated mixture – all these have to be confronted. Failure to deal with death is a major cause of emotional trauma in children, and both mental and physical illness in adults. Dr Elisabeth Kübler-Ross notes that it is quite usual for people who are unable to work through their grief and guilt at the time of a death to become seriously ill afterwards.

If the death is expected due to a terminal illness,

it is very important for both the sick person and his or her family to prepare for it. If the person is willing to discuss the subject, encourage conversation about his or her beliefs. It may be necessary to offer reassurance to terminally ill people if they are afraid. Often it is not death that they are afraid of, but that they might suffer extreme pain beforehand, in which case their medical practitioner should be able to reassure them that the pain will be controlled. Sometimes it is fear of what will happen to the people they love after their death. It may comfort them to know that their dependants will be taken care of afterwards, and that adequate financial provision has been made for them. It may help everyone involved to talk frankly about practical arrangements. Take photographs and videos of the ill person – too often we have a photographic record of major events of our lives, but not this one. It is also important to record the sound of voices – the sound of a much loved voice is often the thing most missed after death. For children it is particularly important to have a tape of their parent's voice, perhaps leaving a message of love and support.

It can be very helpful for those left behind to have a 'memory box'. This can contain small mementoes, photographs, objects closely associated with the person who has died. Barnardo's have found that, in the case of bereaved children, this is particularly valuable to aid the mourning and healing process. Almost any container can be adapted for the purpose, but Barnardo's will supply a specially designed Memory Book and Memory Store – a yellow box with six drawers – by mail order (see address list).

Allow yourself to remember – the bad things as well as the good. Don't feel guilty about grieving; feelings of anger and abandonment after the loss of someone you loved are some of the strongest emotions you are ever going to have to face. Don't feel guilty about not being able to 'think well of the dead' either. If the deceased was a difficult person to get on with or someone who hurt you deeply, the fact of his or her death doesn't alter what he or she was in life. Talk to people about how you feel and about the person you have lost. The healing process can take months or years. Don't let anyone tell you how long it should be. Everyone is different!

If you have children it is vital that you share your grief with them. They too must feel that they have 'permission' to grieve. Let them know that it is natural to be upset. It is too easy to try to hide your own feelings in order to spare others without realising that that inhibits their responses. They may not feel able to show their own feelings unless you do. Dr Kübler-Ross stresses this point in her book *On Death and Dying*. 'The fact that children are allowed to stay at home where a fatality has struck and are included in the talk, discussions, and fears, gives them the feeling that they are not alone in grief and offers them the comfort of shared responsibility and shared mourning. It prepares them gradually and helps them to view death as part of life, an experience that may help them to grow and mature.'

Dr Kübler-Ross writes that children 'are often the forgotten ones. Not so much that nobody cares; the opposite is often true. But few people feel comfortable talking to a child about death.' According to Dr Kübler-Ross, under the age of three a child is 'concerned only with separation'. Up to the age of five death is not perceived as a permanent state. She records the story of the child whose pet dog died: he thought that if he buried his dog, it would one day come up again like the daffodils in spring. From five to ten death is often seen as a 'bogeyman who comes to take people away'. After nine or ten a more realistic conception of death begins to take place and the child will often feel guilt as well as grief and anger. 'They should be listened to, and allowed to ventilate their feelings, whether they be guilt, anger or plain sadness.'

Give those close to the deceased an opportunity to say goodbye. This is particularly important for children, who are often not allowed to see their parent, grandparent or sibling again because they are thought to be too young to see a dead body. It then takes much longer for the death to become 'real' to them and they often feel anger when they are older that they were not allowed to say their own farewells. If the cause of death means that the body is considerably disfigured, remember that a good funeral director can often effect wonderful cosmetic repair. It could be important for the bereaved to be able to touch the body, even if it is just the hand.

It is vital that children should not be lied to. In her book *On Death and Dying* Dr Kübler-Ross writes:

> *children are excluded with the presumption and pretext that it would be 'too much' for them. They are then sent off to relatives, often to the accompaniment of some unconvincing lie that 'Mother has gone on a long trip' or other unbelievable stories. The child senses that something is wrong, and his distrust of adults will only grow if other relatives add new variations to the story, avoid his questions or suspicions, and shower him with gifts as a substitute for a loss he is not permitted to deal with. Sooner or later the child will become aware of the changed family situation and, according to his age and personality, will suffer an unresolved grief that he has no means of coping with. For him, the episode is a mysterious and frightening experience of untrustworthy grownups which can only be traumatic.*

Allow the child to take as much of a part in the preparations as they wish. Children are often more matter-of-fact about death than adults. Sometimes it helps to put a message, or flowers, or a loved object in the coffin with their parent. Above all, let them feel that they have a special part in the ceremony. If it is their mother or father or sibling who has died, they should not be made to feel insignificant or overlooked.

THE DEATH OF A CHILD

The loss of a child is one of the most terrible things that can happen to a parent – it violates the natural order of things and breaks one of the closest possible bonds, causing massive distress. In his book *Funerals and How to Improve Them*, published by Hodder & Stoughton in 1990 but now out of print, Dr Tony Walter writes:

> *It used to be thought that the longer someone lives, the greater the gap when they die. But the death of hopes for the future can cause an enormous gap. . . . When a baby dies, it is not just an individual that has gone; there is a loss of purpose, of expectation, of hope. Our whole understanding of the meaning of life, or marriage, of our love for one another*

disintegrates. . . . When a mother bonds with her baby there is an intense falling in love – and then the object of her love is torn from her. So, when a baby dies before, during or soon after birth, whatever the scientific definition of what has happened, there can be the most massive loss.

For those with religious beliefs it is perhaps easier to comfort the parents with the knowledge that the child has been taken up to heaven by divine purpose, and the secure hope that they will see their child again. For parents who have no religious beliefs it is much harder to make sense of such a terrible event. To compound the loss there may also be feelings of blame or guilt.

A funeral ceremony for a child must somehow help the family to come to terms with these feelings. A sensitive minister will conduct a modified service to take the circumstances into account. For those without religious beliefs, the Humanists have special ceremonies for the loss of a child (see p. 71 below). Children are often buried in white coffins, sometimes covered by a cloth, but in antiquity babies were sometimes interred in rush cradles, perhaps lined with moss, and one archaeological dig revealed a tiny baby laid out on a swan's wing. It is possible to get small alternative containers such as wicker cradles for a child.

Stillbirth, miscarriage and abortion are not generally represented in Western ritual, and yet may leave painful feelings of loss and grief that need to be assuaged. Hospitals will deal with the disposal of the bodies of stillborn children if the parents wish, but it is much better to arrange for your own funeral ceremony. The author Catherine Cookson, whose first child was stillborn, was told that her child could not be buried in its own grave because it had not been baptised. It was interred in the same grave as an elderly woman – something that was common practice until very recently. Catherine said that she felt comforted to know that her child was being held in someone's arms. Cremation is not recommended for a baby, as there are unlikely to be any residual ashes for the parents to collect.

Many cemeteries now also offer burial facilities for babies born before they are regarded as capable of sustaining independent life, but for a very early foetus this may not be practicable. Some ministers may be willing to say prayers for the potential life that was lost, and some Humanist celebrants will conduct ceremonies in these circumstances. New Age and pagan organisations (see address list, under Dragonpaths and the Pagan Federation) also offer sensitive and therapeutic rituals for the acceptance of loss, but it is also possible to devise your own private ceremony.

In the Hebrides and Northern Scotland, there were special ceremonies for stillborn and miscarried babies, whose bodies were wrapped and buried in special places on the mountains. There they became 'children of the rocks' whose spirits could be at peace. On some Pacific islands, small babies were placed in hollowed-out spaces in the trunk of the huge baobab tree that grew in the centre of the village. As the tree continued to grow, it enclosed them within its girth and gradually elevated them higher and higher towards heaven.

THE LEGAL PRACTICALITIES
OF DEATH

The process of registering a death is needlessly complex and bureaucratic, so much so that the DHSS
produces a booklet telling you how to do it. It can
be bewildering for someone going through the process for the first time. The attitude of registrars is not
always as sympathetic as it could be. A friend was very
upset to be greeted by the words 'Are you the widow?'
How much kinder to have asked 'Were you his wife?'

Every death must be registered within five days
(eight in Scotland) by the Registrar for Births,
Marriages and Deaths for the district in which the
death occurred. To do this you will need the medical
certificate of the cause of death, signed by a doctor.
The doctor will also give you a formal notice which
can be given to the Social Services.

If the cause of death was uncertain, it will be referred to the Coroner and the death cannot be registered until the Coroner gives his authority, perhaps only after an inquest has been opened. If the death has been referred to the Coroner, the Coroner's office will advise on the procedures to be followed and issue the appropriate forms.

When you go to the registrar's office you should also take birth and marriage certificates, pension or benefit books (if applicable) and medical cards. The registrar will want to know the date and place of death, home address, date and place of birth and occupation of the deceased, as well as the name, date of birth and occupation of the surviving spouse (if applicable).

The registrar will give you the death certificate (a copy of the entry in the register), a Certificate of Registration of Death to give to the DHSS, and a Certificate for Burial or Cremation (you will need to know which) so that the funeral can be arranged. It is a good idea, before you go, to try to estimate how many copies of the death certificate you will need for insurance companies, banks, probate and so on, as copies are more expensive to order later on. Provided that you can provide suitable storage for the body there is no limit to the length of time that can elapse between the death and the funeral. One woman recently rented cold storage for her husband for six months, so that he could have the burial at sea that he had always wanted. Another family waited three weeks for a sister to arrive from Australia for the funeral.

If you have decided on cremation, you will need to take the third of the certificates mentioned above to the crematorium and obtain application forms: one to be signed by the next of kin and witnessed by a 'responsible householder' who knows the signatory; two cremation forms to be signed by two different doctors (your own doctor will arrange this); and a certificate to be signed by the medical referee at the crematorium. A funeral director should be able to supply these forms for you. Forms need to be returned to the crematorium twenty-four hours before the cremation is due to take place.

All the agencies involved will automatically assume that you have approached a funeral director. If you are going to make your own arrangements you will need to tell them. Don't be put off if you get a slightly negative response – in some areas it is still seen as unusual. If you need help or advice to organise your own funeral, contact the Independent Funerals Advisory Service or the Natural Death Centre (see address list).

ARRANGING A FUNERAL

Ken West, a Bereavement Services Manager who campaigned for a Charter for the Bereaved to be introduced, says that there are three groups whose needs are not being met by the funeral profession: those who want a 'green' funeral; those who want a cheap funeral; or those who simply want something different. In Switzerland, a basic, inexpensive funeral is a civic right – birth and death being the two events over which no one has much choice. In Britain and America the final rite of passage is an unavoidable marketing opportunity. The bill picked up by one's relatives can be something of a shock and the service not always up to the expected standard. If you decide that you want the help of a funeral director, choose carefully – unlike an item of furniture which can be returned to the shop, a funeral happens only once and it has to be absolutely right. A good funeral director can be wonderful, but when things go wrong it only adds to the grief and distress of bereavement.

First of all decide which firms you are going to ask for a quote. Don't be afraid to approach several. Make sure you are dealing with a reputable firm – one does not need a licence to become a funeral director and in theory anyone can set up in business. Many previously sympathetic, family-owned firms are now part of large conglomerates; one particular American chain now controls more than 15 per cent of the British market. Ask for personal recommendations from friends and relatives; if you go through the Yellow Pages or local directories, check whether the firms you have chosen are members of either the National Association of Funeral Directors or the Society of Allied and Independent Funeral Directors. The Natural Death Centre also has a list of recommended firms.

Be aware also that you don't have to use all the services offered by the firm. In some areas it is possible to buy a coffin direct from the local council Bereavement Services office at the cemetery, and arrange for a funeral director to collect the coffin, then collect the body and drive it straight to the cemetery where it can either be kept in cold storage or in the chapel of rest until the funeral service. You can then either have your own choice of bearers to carry the coffin into the ceremonial chapel, hire bearers from the cemetery, or wheel the coffin in on the bier provided. In this way it is possible to have a funeral for less than £400. Arrangements are made through the council's Bereavement Services officer who will sometimes deal with the funeral director for you. There are also a number of firms who offer an alternative service and will do as much or as little as you want them to (see address list).

Before you approach the funeral director it is a good idea to decide what kind of ceremony you want to have and how much money you are able to spend. Do you want a full or a shortened service? Will it be cremation or burial? Do you want a simple, bio-degradable coffin, or a polished wood casket with brass handles? Do you need bearers, or will family members want to carry the coffin themselves? Think carefully about embalming, a chemical process carried out almost routinely these days and often referred to in passing as 'sanitary preparation' or 'hygienic treatment' even 'care of the body' – phrases which few would connect with embalming.

Modern embalming, or 'chemical preservation' is no more effective than refrigeration for preserving the body in the days between death and the funeral and has no effect at all in the long term. Its use is purely cosmetic and is often used by small funeral firms who do not have cold-storage facilities. During the process, the dark blood is drained from the body and replaced by about two gallons of a clear chemical such as formaldehyde. It makes the flesh appear more natural and lifelike and temporarily arrests the shrinking process. Combined with tinted make-up it contributes to the illusion of sleep, or 'life in death'. Not only is it an unnecessary expense, many people are concerned about the environmental effects of these chemicals, not only in the ground, but when released into the atmosphere during cremation. It is also a considerably intrusive interference with the body. If you are Jewish, embalming is strictly forbidden. The only time embalming may be required is for international transportation of the body – some airlines insist upon it.

Remember that arranging funerals can be lucrative for the directors and that however sympathetic the staff, it is in their interests to sell you the most expensive package they can. Telephone for quotes and don't deal with anyone who won't give you prices over the phone. When you have decided on a firm, get a written estimate and insist that there are no hidden extras. This is a legal requirement in the United States. One of the more progressive firms admits that in many cases, the funeral business is 'conducted behind a shroud of secrecy' with the result that a funeral is 'probably the last consumer purchase still being conducted under Dickensian conditions of customer service, presentation and merchandising'. Don't sign up for anything on the spot; go away and think about it in the peace and quiet of your own home. Very often, people don't feel they have the emotional energy to shop around.

The Office of Fair Trading reports that in 97 per cent of cases, people sign up with the first funeral director they contact.

CHECKLIST

The following points may prove useful in deciding what kind of funeral is appropriate:

1. Burial or cremation?
(a) If burial, choice of location? Churchyard? Cemetery? Woodland site? Private site?
(b) If cremation, do you want a particular crematorium?
2. Before the funeral would you like the body kept at home, stored in a mortuary or in a chapel of rest? Will there be an opportunity for relatives to view the body?
3. How would you like the body presented? Dressed in the deceased's own clothes or in a funeral gown?
4. Do you wish it to be embalmed or cosmetically improved? Do you or the deceased's religious beliefs require that relatives are involved in the preparation of the body?
5. Will jewellery be left on the body or given to the next of kin?
6. Are there any medical implants, for example pace makers? This may affect cremation. Hos-

pitals will remove them before releasing the body; if the deceased died at home a doctor or a funeral director must be asked to do so.

7. What type of funeral ceremony would you like, either according to the beliefs of the deceased or the surviving family? Religious? Humanist? New Age? Other? None?

8. What sort of container are you going to have? Basic shroud? Wicker cradle? Carton board coffin? Wood? Veneered chipboard?

9. How would you like the body transported? Stretcher or bier (for walking distance only)? Ordinary estate car? Hearse? Horse and carriage? Special, for example fire engine or lorry? Will relatives want to carry the coffin, or do you need to hire bearers?

10. If the body has been cremated, do you want to collect the ashes afterwards? What kind of container do you want them stored in? Where would you like them scattered?

LIVING WILLS

When someone dies without leaving clear instructions about what kind of funeral he or she would like, it can be more difficult for the relatives to arrange a suitable ceremony. If you have particularly strong views about what is to happen to you when you eventually die, or become terminally ill, it is a good idea to write clear instructions and make sure your relatives know where to find them; alternatively tell the people closest to you what you would like.

You might even consider drawing up a Living Will. This can be deposited with your doctors, your relatives and your solicitor to try to ensure that your wishes are respected. It can be either a simple statement of what you want to happen, what kind of funeral you would like and include an outline of the ceremony; or it can be more formal and define how you would like to be treated if you become terminally ill. Remember that everyone has the right to refuse medical treatment if they wish. The British Medical Association states that 'Competent, informed adults have an established legal right to refuse medical procedures in advance. An unambiguous and informed advance refusal is as valid as a contemporaneous decision.' They recommend a Living Will should be updated every five years. A Living Will is an insurance policy against treatment you would have refused had you been aware of it, being given to you when you are too ill to be consulted. It also ensures that your relatives know what kind of funeral you wanted to have, in the emotional stress of the moment, they may not remember that you told them you were afraid of burial and wanted to be cremated. A legally recognised form of Living Will can be supplied by the Natural Death Centre.

WHAT ARE THE OPTIONS?

For hundreds of year, Western people have dreamt of finding their last resting place in a quiet graveyard within the sound of the church bells. Many inner-city churches have long since run out of space for burial, though some small country communities can still offer this. Others have made space available by clearing very old graves and re-using plots over a hundred years old.

The most popular alternative is to be buried in the local cemetery. Some cemeteries offer an option either for a traditional grave site for those who want a large family memorial, or what is called a 'lawn grave', where the ground is levelled and grassed over so that it can be mown regularly. For the latter, a small headstone, vase or memorial tablet can be placed at the head end of the site on the long, slabbed section dividing the rows of graves. There will probably be a special section for children, and for the burial of cremation caskets.

Recycled graves may be available at a reduced fee for those who do not want a private grave. The site of the grave is usually marked with a small plaque. The body will then be interred in an older, probably Victorian grave, but must be in a biodegradable coffin.

An increasing number of councils are now able to offer a woodland burial site as an option and there are a lot of private sites springing up as this form of burial becomes more popular. This is environmentally very sound, as the tree roots absorb all the decaying material, keeping it from being washed down into the water table. A biodegradable container must be used and obviously it is vital that the body does not contain any embalming fluid, since this would poison the trees. If you like the idea of being buried in a wood with bluebells growing over your grave, this is definitely the right option. If you want something tidy and tended, it would be better to opt for a more traditional cemetery.

Some cemeteries have their own chapels where ceremonies can be held. If members of the family are conducting the ceremony themselves, they must give advance warning to the cemetery authorities.

Some cemeteries have restrictions on the type of container that can be interred. Shrouds are sometimes unacceptable. This may cause distress to groups such as Muslims, who are traditionally buried wrapped in a shroud.

You can also be buried in your own back garden, a farmer's field or on a private plot, providing that it is far enough away from a water supply and does not constitute a change of use of the land (in legal terms, up to two graves have been deemed not to do so). There is no need for planning permission for a single burial, but the location of the grave has to be notified. If you want to be buried in your own garden, bear in the mind the possibility of the house eventually being sold!

CREMATION

Cremation was pioneered in the nineteenth century by Queen Victoria's surgeon, Sir Henry Thompson. The first official cremation in Britain took place on the 26th March, 1885, when a Mrs Pickersgill was cremated at Woking, Surrey, in a crematorium established by the Cremation Society of Great Britain. Today there are more than two hundred crematoria all over the country, handling about half a million cremations a year – 71 per cent of all funerals.

Although cremation is forbidden by Orthodox Jews and Muslims, the Roman Catholic Church

lifted its ban in 1963, and all other Christian denomi-
nations allow cremation. For Sikhs, Hindus and
Buddhists, cremation is part of their traditional rites.

Before you book, ask whether the crematorium has
adopted the Charter for the Bereaved, issued by the
Institute of Burial and Cremation Administration.
This Charter guarantees thirty-three articles which
'define the rights of every individual who experiences
bereavement, and gives the bereaved greater influence over the arrangement of funerals, thereby con-
trolling costs and offering more satisfaction'.
Additional help can be obtained by ringing the
Cremation Society of Great Britain (see address list),
which publishes a free booklet called *What You
Should Know about Cremation*; the society will also
be able to tell you the location of your nearest crematorium. Don't be put off if you find that the crematorium staff are not used to dealing with the public
direct – they are used to making arrangements with
funeral directors and their representatives. This situation is gradually changing as more and more people
want to handle the last rites themselves. But there
is some concern among local government officers
that the traditional system of 'gratuities' exchanged
between funeral directors and staff at crematoriums
and cemeteries leads some staff to discourage
families from doing it themselves. In some areas
gratuities are now forbidden, but in others it is still
a thriving and very lucrative practice.

Most crematorium chapels are non-denominational

and it is possible to decorate them yourself and arrange the seating to your requirements by prior arrangement. Many crematoria allow only twenty to thirty minutes for a ceremony, but it is usually possible to book more time if you want to, although you may be charged extra for this. There is usually an organist and facilities for tapes or CDs, or you can ask live musicians to play; professionals would expect a fee, which they might offer to waive if they were close to the deceased. You might be expected to pay the resident organist if you bring your own. On the other hand, you may not want music of any kind. You can bring your own celebrant or officiate yourself, but if you don't want to do that, the crematorium will have a chaplain who will be happy to conduct the ceremony for you. Some now also provide a 'secular officiant' for those without religious beliefs or you could contact the British Humanist Association. There is, in fact, no obligation to have any kind of ceremony at all.

Most crematoria accept home-made, cardboard, wood, or wicker coffins, shrouds and body bags. All the materials, including handles, must be combustible. If you are using an environmentally friendly container, free from plastic and other pollutants, there may be a reduced fee, since the absence of noxious emissions will allow cremation by only one cremator, rather than the usual two. They may also be willing to hire a trolley to wheel the coffin from the car to the chapel and many will also supply extra bearers, at around £6 each. If the crematorium has cold-storage facilities, it will be possible to book this for a DIY funeral if the body cannot be stored at home, and charges start at around £8 for twenty-four hours.

If you ask beforehand, two relatives can usually be present while the body is being cremated to supervise the committal of the coffin to the cremator. Some crematoria may allow more than two representatives, but space is limited and there are public liability insurance restrictions in some buildings.

The coffin is labelled with a card and this accompanies the body at each stage of the process. According to the Code of Practice, cremation should take place on the same day as the ceremony, not necessarily immediately afterwards, as many people believe. The ashes are later transferred onto a cooling tray, any metal fragments (eg screws or nails) are removed before the remains are reduced to fine powder and placed in an urn. This may weigh between five and seven pounds.

Only one coffin at a time is placed in the cremator, so there is no danger of ashes not being kept separate. If the ashes are not collected by the relatives, the crematorium must keep them for up to a year and then give fourteen days' notice of their intention to dispose of them by strewing or burial.

CRYOGENICS

There has been considerable interest in the idea of freezing either the body or the brain, depending on finances, towards a future date when it becomes scientifically possible to transplant the brain into a new, younger body and provide a 'second life' for the deceased. Apart from being ferociously expensive, there is little evidence that this will ever be a possible form of reincarnation. When an American company was sued because it had got into financial difficulties and the power supply had been cut off, allowing all the stored bodies to thaw, the judge summarily ruled out compensation on the grounds that a return to life was too remote a possibility to be contemplated.

Medical research seems to be much more focused on the technique of cloning, whereby cells from one person can be used to produce another. However, the result is a new individual, not a reincarnation of the parent – like identical twins they are different people even though genetically the same. Cloning human beings, while scientifically possible, is still a long way away in terms of the ethical and moral problems which have to be surmounted first.

ALTERNATIVE UNDERTAKERS

GREEN

There is an increasing number of firms willing to
do both traditional and alternative 'family-centred'
funerals and provide facilities for the rites of non-
Christian ethnic communities. They will offer whatever help the family feel they need, without the
pressure to supply a complete package – offering
everything from a full, traditional funeral service to
simply supplying a coffin and giving informed support. Families are welcome 'to take as much part as
they would like to . . . for instance if they wish to
keep their relative at home, act as bearers, decorate
the coffin, or any other of the tasks called for'. Prices,
even for a complete package, are currently running

at half the national average. Firms such as Green Undertakings, Peace Burials and Funerals Direct are springing up all over Britain (see address list; for a complete list, see *The Natural Death Handbook*). They will sell you a container for the body – anything from carton board to designer coffin – arrange for storage and provide transport to the cemetery or crematorium. They will also help you to lay out the body if you want to and supply a shroud or biodegradable bodybags and wicker stretchers for transporting the body if you wish to do that yourself.

Information on woodland burial sites, how to obtain carton-board coffins and how to arrange inexpensive funerals is available on the Internet, which also has web sites for 'designer dying and celebratory funerals' (see address list).

WOMEN ONLY

An increasing number of people feel revulsion at the thought of a man performing the last, intimate rites for their female relatives. Although many individual funeral directors will provide a woman for the laying-out if requested to do so, there are several all-women funeral services, offering not only basic care of the body, but a complete funeral service if required. Martha's Funerals, Peace Burials and Funerals Direct all offer this service. Information can be obtained from the Independent Funerals

Advisory Service or the Natural Death Centre (see address list).

Regale

According to Regale the shape of the future is a funeral supermarket! The shop, in Walthamstow (see address list), prides itself on taking away the morbidity normally associated with traditional funeral establishments. At Regale you can wander around, choose a coffin, flowers, memorials, price any of the services on offer, hire a hearse or book a complete funeral package. The 'preparation theatre' can be hired for relatives who want to perform the last rites themselves. You are also welcome to go into the shop and just browse! This open approach is refreshing and the marketing policy allows families to involve themselves as much or as little as they wish.

Heaven on Earth

This organisation, in Bristol (see address list), won the Natural Death Centre's award for the Best Funeral Shop and has also won international awards for 'improving the quality of death and dying'. It supplies a wide range of beautifully painted and decorated, environmentally friendly coffins and other funeral regalia. You can be buried in a replica of Tutankhamun's sarcophagus or a Red Arrows Jet, a Ghanaian Fantasy coffin or a Carnival extravaganza of your own design. It also offers help with planning a complete funeral. This can be as conventional or as alternative as you wish. Among its pioneering ideas is that of an 'eternity chest' – a re-usable casket to contain cardboard coffins for later use by members of the family. Prices for a basic, biodegradable coffin made from compacted flakes of spruce, pine and larch start at around £100 but can rise to about £2000 for an elaborate 'Ghanaian Fantasy' design made to order. The standard range of painted and decorated coffins is available for around £300.

DOING IT YOURSELF

There is no mystery about the process of 'laying-out'. It simply means washing and cleaning the body and arranging the limbs and the face in a dignified position before the stiffening process sets in. Rigor mortis sets in about eight hours after death and lasts for about twenty-four hours before the body becomes pliable again and the process of decomposition starts. The eyelids should be closed. Traditionally, a coin was placed on them to stop them opening again. The mouth should be held shut by tying a bandage or a silk scarf lightly under the jaw.

The orifices of the body used to be packed with cottonwool or wadding to prevent the leakage of body fluids after death, but many consider this much too invasive and a breach of dignity. Incontinence pads, which can be bought at any chemist, are frequently used now, and can be changed when necessary. If you don't like the idea of washing and dressing the body yourself, the community nurse is often willing to do it for you.

The body should be kept as cool as possible. In winter it may be sufficient simply to place it in an unheated room. In summer it may be more of a problem. Freezer blocks, sold for picnic hampers, can be used underneath the torso (protected from the skin by a towel or sheet), bags of ice cubes, or dry ice from a local supplier. One family improvised by plugging a fridge in next to the bed and making a tunnel with polythene and parcel tape to keep the body cool. If there is a considerable time delay between the death and the funeral, it may be a good idea to pay for storage facilities at your local crematorium or hospital.

Don't dress the body in the clothes you have reserved for the funeral until just before the ceremony. Wrap the body in a clean sheet, or ordinary night clothes until you are ready. If using a cartonboard coffin, don't place the body in it until the same day, or the evening before at the earliest, and make sure that you put a waterproof sheet and some absorbent material at the bottom of the coffin.

BUYING A CONTAINER

Jane Spottiswoode, in the moving radio documentary about her struggle to organise her husband's funeral – *Undertaken with Love* – argued that self-assembly coffins should be made available at all good DIY outlets. This seems such a sensible idea, it's difficult to say why so many firms threw up their circular saws in horror. You could get a local joiner to make you a simple wooden box, or if you are good at carpentry you could make your own. Full instructions come with *The Natural Death Handbook* and the booklet *How to Direct your own Funeral*. Firms willing to supply coffins direct to the public are listed at the back of *The Natural Death Handbook*, or can be bought from funeral shops. They are sometimes available direct from the local council's Bereavement Services office at the cemetery or crematorium. Self-assembly carton-board coffins are available by mail order (see address list).

Painted caskets are available from funeral shops such as Regale or Heaven on Earth (see p. 194), and carton-board coffins can also be decorated to order, either by yourself or by an artist. A plain box can be covered with an embroidered cloth or quilt – this is usual at royal funerals – and can look quite spectacular.

Wicker cradles are becoming quite popular despite their cost. There is something very comforting about being returned to the earth in a woven basket. The only reservation is that they creak when they are carried, which can be somewhat unnerving during the ceremony.

Many artists and ceramicists make containers for ashes that are more individual and personal than the standard ones supplied by the crematorium. Funeral shops offer them, as do other suppliers (see address list).

ARRANGING TRANSPORT

Many firms will hire out a hearse and driver either on a daily or an hourly rate. If you decide to transport the body yourself, you will need a van or a large estate car – check the measurements carefully. Broom handles or lengths of dowelling on the floor will help the coffin slide in and out easily. If you are using a cardboard coffin, shroud or a biodegradable bodybag you will also need a stretcher. This can be borrowed from the Red Cross or St John's Ambulance, or you can buy one from Green Undertakings (see address list). One family made their own from canvas, using long lengths of dowelling as slot-in handles.

If you want a horse and carriage, these can be hired for funerals just as they are hired for weddings. Check the Yellow Pages for local firms, or if you have a friendly local funeral director they may be willing to put you in contact with the firm that they use.

When you get to the church, cemetery or crematorium, the coffin will either have to be carried by bearers or wheeled on a bier. Some churches and crematoria own them and will lend them out, or a local hospital or health centre may have one it is willing to lend. Otherwise, any sturdy wheeled trolley will do and you may be able to hire one commercially.

If the body is to be buried, you will need strong webbing – upholstery webbing is suitable – to lower the coffin into the ground.

For further help and advice, including information on how to obtain a coffin or find a woodland burial site, see the web sites listed at the end of the book.

THE CEREMONY

Just as it is unnecessary to have a funeral director, so it is not obligatory to have any kind of ceremony at all. A friend of mine said goodbye to her husband in the privacy of their home and then watched him driven off to the crematorium in a plain wooden box, unaccompanied and without flowers or funeral service. Many of her friends and family were scandalised, but it was in accordance with the beliefs that she and her husband had held: 'No flowers. No mourning words.' She collected his ashes a couple of days later and still keeps them with her. She has no regrets.

If you do want a ceremony there are a number of possibilities. You can choose the full rites of whatever religious beliefs you may have, followed by a short service either at the graveside or at the crematorium. If you opt for cremation you can choose to have any kind of ceremony there to fit your own beliefs. You can either book the resident chaplain, or arrange to provide your own minister or 'officiant'.

If you do not have specific religious beliefs there are several excellent organisations who will arrange a ceremony for you. The Humanists and the National Secular Society offer a completely non-religious option; Dragonpaths offers a pagan or New Age alternative; or you could devise your own ceremony which can be as simple or as elaborate as you wish, either religious or non-religious, involving family and friends or not. Unlike marriage, for which there are specific legal requirements about the wording and the location of the ceremony, a funeral rite can take place anywhere and there are no restrictions on the content.

CEREMONIES FOR THE PREPARATION OF THE BODY

In many faiths, such as Islam and Hinduism, washing the body before burial or cremation is an integral part of the rite. The relatives do this for the deceased themselves, and prayers are said over the body. Some funeral directors will allow relatives to prepare the body according to their own religious faith on their premises.

One family, whose father had died after a long

illness, gathered together the night before the funeral to prepare his body for the ceremony. They lit candles to provide soft lighting, poured glasses of his favourite beer, played a tape recording of his favourite Mozart and then carefully washed his body, rubbed perfumed aromatherapy oils into the skin and dressed him in his best suit and tie. They then wrapped him in a linen sheet and lowered him into the coffin where each one kissed him goodbye and said a few words before the lid was screwed in place. Little presents of flowers, tobacco – he had liked to smoke a pipe – photographs of the family and the last of the malt whisky he had kept 'for medicinal purposes', were put into the coffin with him.

One of his daughters said afterwards that, although they had wept a great deal, it had seemed 'so absolutely right'. It would have been easy, she said, 'just to let the funeral firm do it all, but then we wouldn't have been able to say goodbye to Dad properly, and we hated the idea of strangers doing all that to him.'

If you want to look after a loved one yourself there is no problem in arranging such a ceremony if you are keeping the body at home, but if you are using a funeral director, choose an enlightened firm that will let the family perform the 'last rites' themselves.

WAKES

Wakes have a long history and exist in almost every culture. The wake has its origins in the vigil, or watch and was, traditionally, a vigil kept by family, neighbours and friends around the coffin of the dead, either in church or at home. As it has evolved it has become a ceremony for the evening and the night before the funeral service, though the word 'wake' is sometimes applied to the party after the funeral. Candles, fruit and flowers are placed around the room, chairs for the participants, and food and wine as refreshments. In some cultures it is a full-scale party with music, singing, dancing, and readings of poetry and prose. It is a chance for those close to the person who has died to say their last, private farewells. Some organisations, such as Dragonpaths and Peace Burials, will assist families to conduct a wake, and most religious faiths have appropriate prayers to be said for the dead on this occasion. Both the Anglican and the Roman Catholic churches have a liturgy for this. There is also a very good booklet, now out of print, called *Irish Wakes and Amusements*, originally published by Mercia Press in 1989.

BURIAL AT SEA

Although many people love the idea of being slid into the ocean after death, it is now more difficult and expensive to have an ocean funeral. There are only two or three sites around the British Isles where it is permitted. There are other stipulations; the shroud or the coffin must be biodegradable; the body must not be embalmed and must have an identification tag in case it is washed or dredged up again; if a coffin is used it must be drilled with holes to allow water in and must be weighted with about four hundredweight of iron chain or concrete.

The remaining sites are the areas of the channel off Newhaven, and the Isle of Wight. You will need to hire a boat for the purpose and have the permission of the local Fisheries Officer and a free licence from the Ministry of Fisheries and Food. A shipping contact for the Newhaven site is Angus Radford on 01424 424109, and in Poole (for the Isle of Wight) R. H. Bushell on 01202 677539. Details of licences etc can be obtained from the Marine Environmental Protection office of MAFF, on 0171 238 5872. Full instructions are given in *The Natural Death Handbook*. However, permission does not have to be obtained for the scattering of ashes at sea.

For ceremonies, the Anglican church has a variation of the committal for a burial at sea, but for someone without religious beliefs a series of readings of prose and poetry might be appropriate. John Masefield's *Sea Fever* is often used in this context, but his lesser known *Prayer* could easily be adapted.

When the last sea is sailed and the last shallow
    charted,
When the last field is reaped and the last harvest
    stored,
When the last fire is out and the last guest
    departed,
Grant the last prayer that I shall pray, 'Be good
    to me O Lord!'

And let me pass in a night at sea, a night of storm
    and thunder,
In the loud crying of the wind through sail and
    rope and spar;
Send me a ninth great peaceful wave to drown and
    roll me under
To the cold tunny-fishes' home where the drowned
    galleons are.

And in the dim green quiet place far out of sight
    and hearing,
Grant I may hear at whiles the wash and thresh
    of the sea-foam
About the fine keen bows of the stately clippers
    steering
Towards the lone northern star and the fair ports
    of home.

There are a number of appropriate hymns such as 'Eternal Father, strong to save' and 'Lord, in the hollow of Thy hand' (G. W. Briggs). Among other music, Enya's *Orinoco Flow* is popular, while Elgar's *Sea Pictures* include an evocative setting of Richard Garnett's 'Where Corals Lie'; Mendelssohn's *Hebrides* overture, Handel's *Water Music* and Vaughan Williams' *Sea Symphony* all offer suitable associations. Khachaturian's *Spartacus* was used for the television series *The Onedin Line* and, although much used, has a wonderful oceanic feel to it. There is also a large body of folk music associated with seafaring from which to choose.

THEMED FUNERALS

Some people dream of a New Orleans funeral, complete with jazz band and parade; others may want a funeral that has some connection with the interests of the deceased. A lorry driver was recently taken to the crematorium on one of his firm's trucks with an HGV escort which stopped off at his favourite transport café on the way. In West Africa, you can hire an elaborate, decorated coffin to fulfil your fantasies, designs ranging from a Mercedes Benz to a space rocket; the most popular are boats, planes and animals. One man who had made a great deal of money from chicken farming was recently taken to a church in a coffin carved and decorated to resemble a cockerel, and a musician's wife commissioned a piano for her husband. In Britain firms such as Heaven on Earth specialise in supplying decorated, fantasy coffins, but it is possible to paint your own or pay an artist to do so. Themed funerals are also being offered as a package – Peace Burials offer a Railway and a Football Funeral and will create something on request.

Engineers of the Imagination (see address list) will not only arrange for an artist to decorate a coffin, they will also create a special funeral ceremony for you, writing the words, suggesting music, and commissioning other artwork if desired. Since its foundation in 1968, this company has been creating rituals as well as staging large public celebratory events such as lantern and fire festivals all over Britain and Europe. It also runs workshops on how to make funerals 'more personal' which are attended by professionals (funeral directors, medical staff, artists and care workers) and individuals interested in finding out about the possibilities of having a 'creative ending'.

ANGLICAN

The Anglican funeral service is currently under revision. Twenty years ago, the Alternative Services Book was introduced as an interim and is now about to be replaced by a totally new liturgy. The ASB funeral service is widely disliked and rarely used without adaptation. The language has been criticised for being flat, unpoetic and sexist. The new liturgy will allow a blend of material from the old Book of Common Prayer, much loved for its dignified, sonorous language, and new prayers and responses from tried and tested sources.

If the deceased has been resident in the parish, the vicar is obliged to conduct a burial or cremation ceremony if asked to do so. Although in 1997 the Archbishop of Canterbury constructed a wholly individual service for the funeral of Diana, Princess of Wales, parish priests do not have quite so much freedom and are often unwilling to deviate from the liturgy, despite there being no legal requirement (as there is with weddings) to have any particular form of words. Many vicars do allow space for readings and individual tributes. These are particularly important if you want a personal ceremony. Be firm about what you really want. If necessary, find another minister willing to conduct the ceremony.

If you want a particular Anglican minister – other than the vicar of your own parish – to take the funeral ceremony, either in church or at the cemetery, you will have to get permission from your parish priest. This is a courtesy (much like getting your doctor's permission to see another!) and very rarely withheld.

If the deceased is not well known to the vicar, it is a good idea to write a short biography, including all the points that you want him or her to mention and ask the vicar to read it out. This avoids the awful, but all too frequent situation, where the deceased is given the wrong name, and vital details of their lives or relationships are omitted resulting in a bland, anonymous address that could have fitted anyone. If the vicar did not know the deceased at all, try to find someone else who can give the address with affection and conviction. Discuss with the vicar how much time you will be allowed for personal tributes and special readings and where these can be slotted into the ceremony. Talk about the floral decoration of the church, the music you want to use and what the fees are for use of the organ or the choir. If you are providing your own music, this will also have to be agreed.

It is also usual to have printed forms of service which include the hymns and readings and may also have tributes to the deceased and a decorated frontis-piece with names and dates. Sometimes it is possible for the vicar to do this for you on the parish computer (though there will be a charge for printing them out), but you could have them properly printed yourself according to your own design.

Fees for the ceremony will need to be discussed. Many churches have a standard fee for a funeral, but there will be extra costs if either the body or the ashes are being interred in the churchyard. A burial plot will be much more expensive than a small piece of grass to inter a casket of ashes, but prices vary from parish to parish. In some churches it is still possible to be buried in the crypt, but the cost is considerable. It is also possible to have a carved memorial of some kind within the church itself. These can vary from a stone plaque, a carved pew end, a stained-glass window panel or the gift of engraved church furniture – stools, kneelers, candlesticks or wall hangings.

If you have opted for cremation, it is possible to dispense with a separate church service and have the funeral ceremony conducted by the vicar at the crematorium chapel if you wish. You can also arrange with the vicar for the ashes to be interred in the churchyard. The burial of ashes is usually carried out some time after the cremation, in a separate ceremony, and there will be a fee. Most churchyards and cemeteries have separate areas for this. Although most clergy have particular prayers for this occasion – usually a variation of the traditional committal – there is much more scope for creativity here, as long as the vicar agrees. The plot can be marked, but there are usually restrictions on the size of the memorial.

The Anglican funeral service in use at the moment begins with a series of short readings from the Bible, followed by a prayer and then by a psalm. Ask the vicar for a copy so that you can express your own preferences. The Book of Psalms consists of 150 pieces, of which Psalm 23 ('The Lord is my Shepherd') and Psalm 121 ('I will lift up my eyes unto the hills') are often chosen. Then there is a New Testament reading which reminds the congregation of Christ's resurrection and promise of eternal life. There are further prayers and responses. A shortened form of service with slightly different readings is included for the funeral of a child, and there are special prayers for the burial or cremation of a stillborn child.

If the service is held at the crematorium, the committal will follow on straight away – the phrase 'we now commit his/her body to be cremated' being substituted for 'the ground'. If there is to be a burial, the committal will be read at the graveside. The traditional phrase 'earth to earth, ashes to ashes, dust to dust' is now optional. A modified version of the committal is included in the Service Book for the interment of ashes and there is a variation for burial at sea.

There is also provision for the idea of a vigil, or wake. The Alternative Service Book has a service to be read if the coffin is brought into church the night before the funeral, which can also be said at home before the body is taken to church or crematorium. This includes a reading from St Paul's Epistle to the Romans, chapter 8, extracts from Psalms 27 and 139, the Lord's Prayer and a Grace.

ROMAN CATHOLIC

There are three types of ceremony in the Catholic liturgy, depending on the location of the ceremony – at home, in church or at the cemetery. The 'Order of Celebration' is 'common to all liturgical traditions'. There are four elements – the first is a greeting with words of consolation and prayers directed at leading the minds of those assembled towards contemplation of eternal life. There will be an address, which must take into account that there may be people there who rarely attend church and who are unfamiliar with the liturgy. If the ceremony is being held in church there will be communion so that 'the community of the faithful, especially the family of the deceased, learn to live in communion with the one who has "fallen asleep in the Lord", by communicating in the Body of Christ.' Finally the soul of the deceased will be commended to God.

The Byzantine Church has a moving account of this 'last farewell' which is included in the Catholic Catechism:

By this final greeting we sing for his departure from this life and separation from us, but also because there is a communion and a reunion. For even dead, we are not at all separated from one another, because we all run the same course and we will find one another again in the same place. We shall never be separated, for we live for Christ, and now we are united with Christ as we go towards him . . . we shall all be together in Christ.

QUAKER

Quaker funerals are unique for their simplicity and aura of peace. They follow the basic pattern of Quaker meetings for worship, so they can be at the Meeting House or someone's home, at a cemetery, crematorium or the local Quaker burial ground. Friends and family sit round the room, or stand around the grave, and settle into silence, sharing their memories of the dead when they feel moved to do so, praying, offering an appropriate reading, sharing their memories, or remaining silent as they wish.

Until about a hundred years or so ago, when municipal or independent cemeteries were developed, Quakers and other dissenters would not, or could not be buried in the consecrated ground of the established Church. It was therefore necessary for Quakers to be buried on their own land, in their gardens or specially created cemeteries. Many of these are still open today, but are quite full so only Friends or someone with a strong connection are permitted to be buried in a Quaker burial ground.

The following meditation by William Penn (1644–1718), a prominent English Quaker and the founder of Pennsylvania, is often read at Quaker funerals. It comes from *Quaker Faith and Practice*, an anthology of Quaker writing.

And this is the Comfort of the Good,
that the grave cannot hold them,
and that they live as soon as they die.
For death is no more
than a turning of us over from Time to
Eternity.
Death, then, being the way and condition of
Life,
we cannot love to live,
if we cannot bear to die.

They that love beyond the World, cannot be
separated by it.
Death cannot kill what never dies.
Nor can Spirits ever be divided
that love and live in the same Divine
Principle,
the Root and Record of their Friendship.
If Absence be not death, neither is theirs.

Death is but Crossing the World, as Friends do
the Seas.

HUMANIST

If you do not have any particular religious beliefs and do not feel up to conducting a funeral yourself, a Humanist ceremony may be the best option. These ceremonies can take any form and, by discussion with the celebrant, personal tributes, favourite readings and music can be incorporated.

The extract below comes from a ceremony, followed by burial, that was conducted for a very small child.

Friends, we meet here today to celebrate the life of Susan Jones. (Please be seated.)

This is a sad day, especially sad because grief for the loss of a child is hardest to bear. When an old person dies we may grieve, but we can accept more readily that a life has been lived and has drawn to its inevitable close. But when a child dies, we mourn not only the life that was, but also the life that might have been. It is right and natural that we should grieve, because sorrow is a reflection and measure of the love, the happiness and the intimacy we shared with the one who has gone. In a way too, we grieve for ourselves, because we know that our own lives will never be the same without her.

Inevitably you will find the world a poorer place without Susan, but it will always be a richer place because she was once in it. So the joy of having a daughter, a granddaughter, a sister, a niece, a young friend, may indeed be lost; but the joy of having had that relationship, the delight and comfort of its memories, is never lost. There never has been and never will be anyone in the world like Susan, and she will live in your memories not just at special times like birthdays, but always. She will always remain a part of the family.

So we are here not just to mourn, but also to celebrate Susan's life. It was of course, a very short life, but I would like to suggest to you that our habit of measuring the worth or the quality of a life by its duration is a bad one. Time does not bring out what matters most in life. I can best illustrate what I mean by quoting the words of two very different writers. First the great Russian novelist Alexander Solzhenitsyn, who wrote:

Some people are bound to die young. By dying young a person stays young for ever in people's memory. If he burns brightly before he dies, his light shines for all time.

And the sixteenth-century dramatist Ben Jonson wrote:
A lily of a day
Is fairer far in May.
Although it fall and die that night
It was the plant and flower of light.

It is the enduring brightness of Susan's life that I now want us to reflect.

[There followed a tribute to Susan, an account of her short life and a moment of silent contemplation, where those who had a religious faith were invited to make their own private prayers. The celebrant then said a few closing words and thanked those present for their support for Susan's parents. The ceremony closed with music chosen by the parents.]

The Committal

My friends, we have been remembering with sadness yet with warm appreciation, the short life of Susan Jones. She is now beyond harm, fear and pain; and here – in this last rite – we commit her body to the safe bosom of our Earth, which sustains and regenerates all life.

The memory of her life and personality we shall cherish with love and gratitude. As we return to our homes, to our work, to our lives, let us resolve to follow Susan's example by using our lives more fully and to better purpose, with the same cheerfulness and determination that were so much a part of Susan's life.

I now invite those close to Susan to place their flowers as I have done, before we take our leave. Thank you, my friends.

JEWISH

Most Jews today believe that after death 'The spirit of man returns to God, who gave it.' Devout Jews hope to be able to recite the Shema before the moment of death. If they are too weak to do so, someone has to say it for them. 'Shema' means 'hear', and is the beginning of a prayer that Jewish people learn during childhood.

Hear, O Israel; the Lord our God, the Lord is One.
And thou shalt love the Lord thy God with all thine
heart, and with all thy soul, and with all thy might.

The Tziddukha-Din should be said at the moment of death. Someone, usually a close male relative, must remain with the dead, and psalms are recited over the body, which is wrapped in a white sheet and laid on the floor with a lit candle at the head.

Funerals are traditionally simple affairs. Jews believe that we should go out of this life equal, as we came into it. Funerals should take place within twenty-four hours of the death wherever possible. The Jewish community does not usually have professional undertakers. 'It is a voluntary honour to assist in the burial of the dead.' Most Jews will belong to a 'burial society' and fellow members perform the last offices and preparation of the body. At the service, mourners may uninhibitedly tear their clothes as a sign of grief, and the Kaddish, a prayer of thanksgiving, is recited in memory of the dead person by his or her sons. In the Reform movement, daughters may also say Kaddish. Orthodox Jews must be buried, but Reform Jews allow cremation. The body is dressed in a white shroud and, if a man, must wear his prayer shawl, ritually torn to prevent it being worn again by anyone else. Most Jews are buried in private cemeteries belonging to the burial society they had joined. All the men at the ceremony must cover their heads, whether Jewish or non-Jewish, and close male relatives help to fill in the grave.

It is traditional for the family to eat a bread roll and a boiled egg as symbols of continuing life, before the funeral meal is served for all those who attended. After the funeral there is usually a week of private mourning, known as *shiva* (the seven days), during which the family are supposed to sit on low stools or on the floor and abstain from all kinds of activity including bathing, cutting their hair and having sex. This is intended to give the bereaved the opportunity to mourn properly before re-entering everyday life. On the anniversary of the death, children light a candle and recite Kaddish at the synagogue.

BUDDHIST

There are several types of Buddhism, with slightly different ceremonies surrounding death. Buddhists believe that death is a transitional state between one life and another. It is important for the dying person to be prepared for death in order for the soul to pass through the door ready for the next stage of rebirth. The state of mind at the time of death is crucial, because this determines the situation that person will be born into. If there is time, it will be possible to have a spiritual guide to assist in the last rites.

In Tibetan Buddhism the dying person should be encouraged to recite the Three Refuges, or have it recited for them if they are too weak, followed by a prayer of dedication.

Wholly and without reserve I dedicate myself to the company of the Enlightened and their spiritual sons. Take possession of me. With humility I offer myself as your servant. Having become your property I have nothing more to fear in this world. . . . Through hatred and infatuation I have done many wrong things. I have not realised that I am only a traveller passing through this world. Day and night, without cessation, vitality decreases and death approaches.

This should be followed by recitation of the Ten Precepts and a prayer called the Heart of Perfect Wisdom, which should be repeated until the very last breath has been taken. This should still be done over the body even if death is sudden or accidental, with no time for preparation. The prayers and spiritual intercession of the living is crucial to aid the passage of the soul.

Buddhists are traditionally cremated and the blazing flames consume all the impurities of the body. Chinese Buddhists often prefer to be buried and the dead are laid in the coffin wearing their shoes. The content of the ceremony will depend slightly on the type of Buddhist teaching followed by the deceased, and the celebrant is usually the person who has acted as their spiritual guide.

Tibetan Buddhists suggest that an altar should be

erected in the room where the funeral ceremony is to be held. This should hold a photograph of the deceased, an image of the Buddha, candles and offerings of flowers, food and incense. There should also be a jug of water and a bowl standing in a tray, so that when water is poured, any spillage will be contained.

The British Buddhist Association has a printed order of service for a memorial, funeral or cremation, which it will supply on request. This begins with reflections on death in prose and poetry, and the recital of the Wheel of Life, Death and Rebirth. Then there are readings from Buddhist teaching, including the story of Kisa Gotami, followed by the chanting of the Homage, the Three Refuges and the Praise of the Triple Gem. The Five Precepts of Buddhist life are recited and then there is a short appreciation of the life of the deceased.

The ceremony of the charging of the water follows, while those assembled chant the following prayer:

As water runs from rivers to fill the ocean
So may wellbeing and merit within us
Pour forth and reach our departed one,
Who may thus be filled therewith
And share these thoughts with us.

By the power of the Master may s/he be well and
  happy;
By the power of Truth may s/he be well and
  happy;

*By the power drawn from us may s/he be well and
    happy;*
*By the power of the Triple Gem may s/he attain
    Nirvana!*

At this point the coffin is committed for either cremation or burial with a prayer that begins:

Here nothing is; only a worn-out thought,
*Whose parent mind thinks elsewhere thoughts
    anew.*
Here's but the ashes of a garment wrought
With mental fingers by the living you.

Life only is, life the unceasing womb,
Whose children move the cycles of their day
And jest awhile; within the closing tomb
*There's nought but dust new settled by the
    way.*
The world is but a grave wherein we find
Only the drifting shadows of pure mind.

Flowers are strewn on the coffin as more prayers are
read and the final farewell:

Farewell, friends! Yet not farewell;
Where I am, ye too shall dwell.
I am gone before your face
A heart-beat's time, a grey ant's pace.

Yet when ye come where I have stepped,
Ye will marvel why ye wept.

For Tibetan Buddhists the ceremony is slightly different and includes private prayer and meditation. The celebrant opens the ceremony with a tribute to the dead and a prayer is then recited three times.

O Buddhas and Bodhisattvas, abiding in all
  directions,
endowed with great compassion,
endowed with fore-knowledge,
endowed with the divine eye,
endowed with love, affording protection to sentient
  beings,
condescend through the power of your great
  compassion to come forth;
condescend to accept these offerings concretely laid
  out and mentally created.

O Compassionate Ones, you who possess the
  wisdom of understanding,
the love of compassion, the power of doing divine
  deeds
and of protecting in incomprehensible measure;
[name] is passing from this world to the next.
S/he is taking a great leap.
The light of this world has faded for her/him.
S/he has entered solitude with his karmic forces.

S/he has gone into a vast Silence.
S/he is borne away by the Great Ocean.

O Compassionate Ones, let not the force of your
    compassion be weak, but aid her/him.
Let him not go into miserable states of existence.
Forget not your ancient vows.[1]

As in the British Buddhist ceremony, a narrative from the scriptures is read, and frequently this includes the story of Kisa Gotami (see p. 154 below). The Heart of Wisdom is repeated and the Five Vows. At a suitable point in the service, indicated by the priest, a relative pours water symbolically from the jug into the bowl. The litany of the flowers from the *Tibetan Book of the Dead* is read as the mourners place flowers on the coffin:

flowers, yellow flowers, black flowers,
all the different kinds
of the colours of flowers,
all of the different kinds
of love's shining-forth . . .

There is death and life,
there is no death, no life.
There is changing life, there is unchanging life.
There is nirvana, there is samsara.

[1] *Tibetan Book of the Dead*, Oxford University Press.

Clouds change into multitudinous forms.
Water changes form as it wishes,
taking the shape of its container.
Flowers change colour, moment by moment.

Such a vivid world! Such a bright you!
You were born out of these flowers,
you gave birth to these flowers.
You have no beginning and no ending,
You are bottomless and limitless,
even as also you are infinitesimal dust.

You are love. You are the flower.

Tibetan Buddhists believe that the soul remains in transition for forty-nine days and relatives offer prayers and food and light candles for the dead every seventh day in order to assist its passage. The forty-ninth day is particularly important. A year after the death there is a special ceremony and feast to mark the rebirth of the soul.

MUSLIM

For followers of Islam, as with many other faiths, death is the end of life on this earth and the beginning of a life hereafter. For Muslims 'Death is not final, but a temporary separation from the beloved person, who will be brought back to life on the Day of Judge-

THE CEREMONY

ment and, if God wills, be reunited with his family once more.'[2]

Muslims' particular requirements for the burial of the dead are often not met outside Islamic countries, and the necessity for them not understood within local communities. In Britain the Commission for Racial Equality has published a paper outlining measures that need to be taken by local authorities which also makes recommendations for central and local government. Some local councils have acted upon this advice and provide separate burial facilities in their cemeteries for non-Christians, but others still do not make any special provision and this sometimes leads to unnecessary distress for relatives.

The Holy Prophet urged Muslims to bury their dead quickly and it is traditional to bury the deceased within twenty-four hours. This can be difficult when death occurs at the beginning of a weekend or before a bank holiday and it is impossible to register the death and obtain the necessary certificates in time. It is also necessary to have the grave prepared in a particular way so that it is aligned towards Mecca, ie on a north-east to south-west axis. The body is placed in the grave so that the head is at the south-west end, facing towards Mecca.

The body must be ceremonially washed before burial and this is sometimes done at the graveside, if a standpipe is available. Lack of suitable washing

[2] Commission for Racial Equality

facilities in cemeteries has led to this ritual being done in the mosque. Many new mosques have a special section for this, although it requires special permission from the local authority. The funeral prayer Salat Al-Janazah is said while the body is being washed, either at the mosque or at the graveside. The body is then wrapped in one or two sheets of white cloth and laid in the grave. It is not traditional to have a coffin, although some people now do so.

The finished grave must be raised from the ground between four and twelve inches, to prevent anyone walking or sitting on it, as this is strictly forbidden. The levelling of graves, practised in many cemeteries to make them easier to maintain, is also forbidden by the Muslim faith. There must be only one body in the grave and a simple headstone.

Failure to understand these requirements often causes offence which could easily be avoided by setting aside an area within the cemetery for Muslim burials and either having a Muslim on the cemetery staff or allowing families to dig their own graves. Lack of local facilities and unsympathetic staff have led many Muslims to undertake the expense of flying the body back to Asia or the Middle East for burial. The situation is improving, and there are now several private cemeteries providing the proper facilities and many more local councils will allow Muslims to dig their own graves.

HINDU

It is the desire of all devout Hindus to die beside the Ganges and be cremated at the Burning Ghats in Varanasi. The body is carried, wrapped in a white shroud, by bearers chanting the name of God. It is first washed in the river and some of the water sprinkled into the mouth. Piles of sandalwood are sold for the pyre and the sacred fire is obtained from the priest Yama, the god of death. Relatives have to light the pyre five times with the ritual fire. When the cremation is over, the ash is swept into the river Ganges and marigold petals are tossed in with it. Families in Britain who cannot afford to have the body of their relative flown back to India often take the ashes back to be ritually sprinkled into the Ganges at a later date.

Hindus generally believe in reincarnation. Funeral rites are about directing the soul towards a better life. If the proper rites are not observed, there is a danger of the soul being trapped in limbo. If possible, a Hindu should die on the ground, or as close to it as he or she can get. Dying people will often struggle out of bed in defiance of hospital or nursing home staff in order to lie on the floor. After death, the body is placed on the floor and a special candle made from flour and ghee placed at the right side of the head. Particular mantras are recited and passages from the *Bhagavad Gita*.

The body is covered with flowers, a floral wreath placed about the neck and sandalwood paste smeared on the forehead. A small amount of water from the river Ganges is poured into the mouth and sometimes a symbolic fire of sandalwood, or some other perfumed wood is lit in the room.

Just before the funeral, the body is washed and dressed by relatives of the same caste. The clothes are supposed to be new, but a woman is usually dressed in her wedding sari. Cremation should follow within twenty-four hours of the death, but this is not always practicable in Britain. A Hindu priest usually conducts the ceremony, which involves the recitation of fifteen mantras, but in some areas it may not be possible to find a priest. In this case relatives try to find someone of high caste who knows the mantras. The funeral is followed by a period of ritual mourning which lasts about two weeks when relatives empty the room of furniture and cover the floor with white sheets, sitting on the floor to receive visits of condolence.

NEW AGE PAGAN

The word 'pagan' encompasses a wide range of beliefs, ranging from the New Age movement, through Celtic shamanism and Wicca, to the re-created rites of the Druids. Pagans often decide to be buried for environmental reasons, so that the body can go back to the earth to nourish new life. Woodland burial has become very popular.

When Jenny died, aged thirty-four, in a car accident, her devastated relatives realised that – whatever their own beliefs – a conventional funeral service would be totally inappropriate. She had always been an independent free-spirited person and her family and friends wanted a funeral which would have room for their grief while also being a celebration of Jenny's life. Jenny had no religious beliefs but did have a strong spiritual connection to the earth and Nature, and her family felt that it was very important to acknowledge this. Annie Wildwood, of Dragonpaths, was asked to coordinate the arrangements and be the celebrant. On her advice a local funeral director was asked to store Jenny's body to give the family time to decide what sort of funeral service they really wanted.

Jenny's partner, David, wanted her to have a nature reserve or woodland burial, as he knew that this is what she would have preferred. None of the family liked the idea of using a conventional coffin; it was ugly, expensive and wasteful. In the end they chose a biodegradable bodybag which they could decorate. Jenny's mother and her two young nieces (aged eleven and nine) covered the plain cotton bag with appliquéd flowers, stars, animals, birds and geometrical shapes, using bright fabrics, ribbons, beads, sequins and fabric paints. Others wrote messages on the bag. It became a unique and beautiful cocoon for Jenny to rest in.

Fortunately there was a woodland burial site close to Jenny's home and her family was able to go and look at it and choose a plot. Jenny's brother Alan and some of their friends washed and cleaned his elderly Volvo estate to transport the body, putting a thick layer of new-mown hay in the back – a smell which Jenny had loved. A flat wooden pallet with rope handles was provided to support the bodybag when carrying it. The day before the funeral, Alan and some of Jenny's friends brought the body home, resplendent in its colourful cocoon. People wanted to be able to sit in silence with the body; the curtains were closed and the soft glow of candlelight lit the room, which had previously been blessed by the celebrant. An oil-burner released the gentle scent of lavender and people commented on the sense of sacredness about the room and a deep feeling of peace.

On the day, everyone travelled down to a pub near the burial site. A marquee had been erected in the pub gardens, which were quite large and secluded. People brought tables, chairs, cloths, cutlery, dishes, and a wonderful variety of food and drink – a real joint effort to which people seemed very glad to be able to make their own contributions. Jenny's body was laid on a bier at one end of the marquee (actually a set of milk-crates covered by a colourful African cloth). Nearby was a memorial table, upon which were photographs, candles and other objects to commemorate Jenny's life, including her old teddy bear, a statue of a horse (she had loved horses), some favourite books, her walking boots, bright yellow chrysanthemums and some of her favourite jewellery.

The family wanted as little formality as possible, though there was a rough timetable. It had been debated whether or not to allow children to take part in the gathering, but the consensus was strongly in favour of inviting them to do so if they wished. The very little ones treated it as some sort of party and played outside for most of the time; those who were old enough to understand what was happening appreciated being given the choice. Everyone sat in a circle, with Jenny's body at the north side. People had brought poems, songs, excerpts from books, reminiscences, memories, accounts of episodes they had shared with Jenny. Some simply spoke of their feelings, or did not speak at all. Several expressed deep and bitter anger at the suddenness and untimeliness of Jenny's death. Afterwards there was eating, drinking, talking and weeping as well as laughter.

The team of bearers took turns carrying the body on the half-mile journey to the burial site and everyone else followed. There was a spontaneous sense of solemnity among the gathering; people fell silent or murmured quietly. Then someone began singing 'Swing low, sweet chariot' and others joined in. It was all powerfully moving. At the graveside Jenny's body was carefully lowered with ropes onto newmown hay from the car. Some people threw flowers into the grave and the celebrant recited a short blessing, commending Jenny's body to the rich earth and her spirit to the wild wings of the north wind.

The grave was filled in by many helping hands and finally Jenny's parents and David planted a small beech tree. As dusk was falling most people returned to the marquee, but some remained behind with candle-lanterns, a guitar and wine. 'We're going to sit with her a bit and sing her to sleep', one of them said. Participants afterwards remarked on the 'natural rightness' of all that had happened. Jenny's sudden and tragic death had left a great deal of shock, pain and anger, but the love her friends and family felt for her and the certainty that they had done their best for her seemed to run through the events of the day like a bright thread in a tapestry, leaving behind the knowledge that they had created something truly meaningful to mark Jenny's presence among them.

DRUID

Funerals are called 'parting ceremonies', and Druids believe that death is a gateway into the spiritual world. The ceremony is both a celebration of the new life the soul has been born into as well as the life that the person led on earth. Philip Carr-Gomm describes such a ceremony held on the isle of Iona for Lucie, who died aged only seventeen. This is only a brief extract from a longer account of Lucie's life and was interspersed with music by Kate Bush and Enya.

O Great Spirit – Mother and Father of us all, we ask for your blessing on this our ceremony of thanksgiving and honouring and blessing of Lucie.

We stand at a gateway now, a gateway that each of us must step through at some time in our lives. Lucie has stepped through this gateway already. Her soul is immersed in the shining light of the Unity that is the mother and father of us all.

The sadness and the pain that we feel now is in our knowledge and our experience of the fact that we ourselves cannot yet cross that threshold to be with her until our time has come – until we too can begin what has been described as the Great Adventure. . . .

O Great Mother of all Being, we give thanks for what is given, we give thanks for what is taken. Even though we do not understand. Even though we do not understand.

. . . Dear Lucie, may your journey to the Isles of the Blessed, to the centre of God, to the land of freedom and splendour, be swift and sure. . . .

We ask that the blessing of the Spirits of the Tribe and of the Ancestors, of Time and of Place and of the Journey be with you.

We ask that the blessing of the Spirits of North and South, East and West be with you. We ask that you might be blessed with Fire and with Water, with Earth and with Air and with Spirit.

We ask for the blessing of the Lord and Lady of the Animals and the Woods, the Mountains and the Streams.

We ask that the blessing of the Uncreated One, whose Son and Daughter are the Created Word, and of the Spirit that is the Inspirer, may be always with you.

And in silence now we send Lucie our own blessings for a safe and joyous life in the Other World – filled with peace and clarity and love.

By the beauty of the fields, the woods and the sea, by the splendour that is set upon all that is, we send you our own love and blessings, dear Lucie.

As the sun rises in the east and sets in the west, so too are each of us born and so too do each of us die. But as the sun returns anew each day, so too do we return to earth, refreshed and renewed. Dear Lucie, know that just as you have been born into the spiritual world, so too will you be born again on earth – when it is right, in your own time. Now go safely, go well, go surely. Our hearts are with you. There is no separation.

Fare Thee well, Lucie.

The full ceremony is included in *The Druid Way* by Philip Carr-Gomm.

THE SCATTERING OF ASHES

Often families feel that it is appropriate to scatter ashes in places that had a particular association with the dead person. My uncle's ashes were scattered on his favourite mountain, another member of the family chose to have hers dug into a much-cherished rosebed. In theory you are supposed to have permission to scatter ashes on someone else's land or in public access places, but in practice (since ashes are sterile and no risk to public health) people rarely seek official sanction. A crematorium will often have a garden of remembrance where the remains can be scattered, but the site has to be shared with many other people, and families sometimes want a more individual focus for grief. A northern pub recently offered niches for the caskets of real ale devotees – the nearer to the bar the more expensive the slot! It is also possible to arrange to have a very small quantity of ash (a token amount) sprinkled onto your favourite football or cricket pitch, if you can get the club to agree. The most popular locations for ash scattering are in the open air, either mountain, coast or woodland. One man arranged for some of his ashes to be made into fireworks to be lit at his funeral celebration! It is also possible for the ashes to be separated into several small containers and scattered in different locations.

If you have always dreamt of a burial at sea, but

find that it is impractical or too expensive, it is relatively easy to arrange for ashes to be scattered and you do not have to have permission. This can be done from the rocks on the shoreline, or from a boat further out at sea. The committal ceremony might include the floating of wreaths, or single flowers out onto the water, and paper boats with lighted candles. Make sure that everything is biodegradable and won't end up on the beach in a tidemark of refuse.

The ceremony can be as large or small as you want it to be. You can invite guests, or just the immediate family; have a beach barbecue or a quiet meal in a pub. Some people prefer to have a public funeral ceremony and keep the final committal strictly private. Carol, whose husband died when he was only in his thirties, scattered his ashes alone in the woods where he had proposed to her and where they had often loved to walk. She took a picnic and a bottle of wine and read some poetry aloud. It was a deeply private experience that she could not have shared with anyone else.

For the content of the ceremony, there is a wide variety of readings, prayers and blessings that can be read out. Someone may want to say a few words about the life of the deceased, or you may want to observe a few moments' silence in his or her memory. You could have a celebrant to conduct the ritual and a solo instrument such as a flute, clarinet, harp, guitar or bagpipes to play the soul on its journey. Most of the words of committal in traditional funeral rites can be adapted for the scattering of ashes and there are a number of suitable secular pieces included in the anthology at the end of this book.

The following order of ceremony was put together for Mary Baker, a woman in her sixties who died of cancer. Only close family and a few friends were there for the scattering of ashes, standing in a group at the bottom of her garden, where the ceremony was conducted by a family friend. The music, including Butterworth's *English Idyll No. 2*, was played on a portable tape recorder, operated by a member of the family.

Celebrant:

Friends, we've gathered here today to scatter Mary's ashes. This is our last chance to say a final farewell to a very special person who was much loved by all who knew her. Mary always said that when she died she didn't want any fuss and that if it was possible she'd like her ashes scattered in the garden she created out of a wilderness when she and Tom bought this house – the garden she loved to sit and look at when she became too ill to do any more work in it. Most of the plants that you can see here were put in by Mary and are a living memorial to her skill and dedication. Mary was one of the best friends I could ever have had and I miss her dreadfully.

Now Anne [Mary's niece] would like to read something, and then afterwards Jake [Mary's son] will say a few words.

Anne:

> *To every thing there is a season, and a time to every purpose under the heaven;*
> *A time to be born, and a time to die; a time to plant, and a time to pluck up that which is planted;*
> *A time to hurt, and a time to heal; a time to break down, and a time to build up;*
> *A time to weep, and a time to laugh; a time to mourn, and a time to dance;*
> *A time to cast away stones, and a time to gather stones together; a time to embrace, and a time to refrain from embracing;*
> *A time to get, and a time to lose; a time to keep and a time to cast away;*
> *A time to rend, and a time to sew; a time to keep silence and a time to speak;*
> *A time to love and a time to hate; a time of war and a time of peace.*
> *To every thing there is a season, and a time to every purpose under heaven.*

Ecclesiastes, chapter 3, verses 1–8

Jake:

> *I just want to say how much I appreciated all the things she did for me even though I didn't always show it the way I should have done. She was a wonderful Mum – the best.*

Celebrant:

Tom [Mary's husband] doesn't feel up to reading anything himself, so he asked me to read this for him:

Death is nothing at all. . . . I have only slipped away into the next room. I am I and you are you. Whatever we were to each other that we are still. Call me by my old familiar name, speak to me in the easy way which you always used. Put no difference in your tone; wear no forced air of solemnity or sorrow. Laugh as we always laughed at the little jokes we enjoyed together. Play, smile, think of me, pray for me. Let my name be ever the household word that it always was. Let it be spoken without effort, without the ghost of a shadow on it. Life means all that it ever meant. It is the same as it ever was; there is absolutely unbroken continuity. Why should I be out of mind because I am out of sight? I am waiting for you for an interval, somewhere very near, just around the corner. All is well.

Henry Scott Holland, Death is Nothing at All, from *Facts of the Faith*

Now I'm going to ask Jake and Tom to scatter Mary's ashes in this corner of the garden and then they're going to plant a Japanese cherry tree as a memorial.

[During the scattering of ashes and the tree planting, a tape recording of Vaughan Williams's *The
Lark Ascending* was played and the celebrant read
the following two poems]:

Sleeping at last, the trouble and tumult over,
  Sleeping at last, the struggle and horror
   past,
Cold and white, out of sight of friend and of lover,
  Sleeping at last.

No more a tired heart downcast or overcast,
  No more pangs that wring or shifting fears
   that hover,
Sleeping at last in a dreamless sleep locked fast.

Fast asleep. Singing birds in their leafy cover
  Cannot wake her, nor shake her the gusty
   blast.
Under the purple thyme and the purple clover
  Sleeping at last.

Christina Rossetti, *Sleeping at Last*

Farewell to Thee! But not farewell
To all my fondest thoughts of Thee;
Within my heart they still shall dwell
And they shall cheer and comfort me.

Life seems more sweet that Thou didst live
And friends more true that Thou wert one;

Nothing is lost that Thou didst give.
Nothing destroyed that Thou hast done.

Anne Brontë, *Farewell*

After the tree had been planted, everyone stood quietly for a few moments, saying their own private farewells to Mary. Then the celebrant read the following short extracts:

The wise in heart mourn not for those that live, nor those that die. Never the spirit was born; the spirit shall cease to be never. Never was time the spirit was not. End and Beginning are dreams! Death hath not touched it at all, dead though the house of it seems! Nay, as when one layeth his worn-out robes away, and, taking new ones, sayeth, 'These will I wear today!' so putteth by the spirit lightly its garb of flesh, and passeth to inherit a residence afresh.

Bhagavad Gita

So be my passing!
My task accomplished and the long day done,
My wages taken, and in my heart
Some late lark singing,
Let me be gathered to the quiet west,
The sundown splendid and serene.

W. E. Henley, *Meditation*

CREATING YOUR OWN FUNERAL CEREMONY

The first thing to establish is what kind of ceremony you want. Religious or secular? Formal or informal? What kind of beliefs did the deceased have, and how does this fit in with the wider family context? This may determine the mixture of elements within the ceremony.

Where are you going to hold it? You can legally hold a funeral ceremony anywhere. Will it be in a church, chapel, pub, hotel function room, private house, garden, seashore, woodland glade, cemetery, in a football club, on a steam train or a boat? If the ceremony is not going to be in the same place as the burial or cremation, you will need to organise suitable transport from one location to the other.

Who is going to be the celebrant? Bear in mind that it must be someone confident, dignified and sensitive enough to keep his or her composure through the ceremony and support others through it.

How much of a part are family and friends going to play? They may want to offer tributes to the dead, or simply read a poem or prose piece. For a crematorium or church ceremony you will need to make sure these are kept short in order not to overrun the time-slot. If members of the family don't feel up to reading anything in public, they may want to light a candle, help to carry the coffin or place the flowers round it.

Draw up an order of service, listing the different elements of the ceremony and the names of the participants, showing clearly what each person will be doing. If you are using music, time each piece and indicate where in the ceremony you want it to be played.

Are you having live music, or taped? If you are using an organist they will need to know well in advance what they are to be required to play, the cues and the duration. This applies to the person operating the CD or tape player. For coming in and going out, make sure the music is long enough to prevent people filing in and out in silence.

How are you going to arrange the seating and decorations? Are the chairs going to be in formal rows or in a friendly circle? If it is fixed, for example as in church pews, are you gong to decorate the ends with evergreens and flowers? Other decorative elements could include lanterns, candles, banners, photographs and floral displays. Do you want the coffin to be covered by a cloth? If not, will it be painted or just bare wood with flowers placed on it?

If the ceremony is to be held at a crematorium, you will need to decide whether you want the coffin to disappear behind curtains, or be lowered out of sight at the end of the ceremony. You can opt to keep it in view until everyone has left, so that people can pay their last respects on the way out.

If the ceremony is at the graveside, you will need to decide whether you want something to cover the earth that has been dug out. This is usually plastic grass – if you don't want this, you will have to organise something else such as rush matting, or leave the earth uncovered. At the end of the ceremony, do you want family members and friends to throw the traditional shovelful of earth into the grave, or walk away leaving it open? If you want to fill it in either completely or partially, you will need to provide some shovels.

CUSTOMS AND SYMBOLS
ASSOCIATED WITH FUNERALS

The dead are traditionally carried into church feet first with the idea that they can see where they are going. If this was done, it was believed that their souls were less likely to haunt the living. It was also thought that when someone died, the window of the room should be opened to speed the flight of the soul to heaven. The release of birds (often doves) at a funeral symbolises the release of the human soul.

Black is associated with absence – the darkness that results from the absence of light – and therefore often has negative associations. Traditionally it is the colour of mourning in the West; white, its opposite, is the mourning colour in many other cultures, including Buddhism.

Certain trees have traditional links with death and

mourning. Cherry blossom is the Chinese symbol of immortality: the wood is supposed to defend against evil spirits and an arcade of cherry trees was the gateway to the afterlife. Cypress trees and other long-lived evergreens such as yew were traditionally planted beside Christian graves to symbolise eternal life. The ancient Greeks also associated the cypress with death and burial and in Greek mythology several gods and goddesses have it as their symbol. As Feste sings in *Twelfth Night* 'Come away, come away Death/And in sad cypress let me be laid' (Act II, scene 4).

Laurel, the symbol of victory, had the additional property of being able to cleanse the soul from guilt in Greek and Roman mythology. Laurel groves were grown around most Greek sacred sites. In early Christian belief laurel wreaths were a symbol of victory over death, and they often accompanied the coffin to its final resting place. In Britain, the weeping willow is the tree of mourning. It is now possible to buy coffins woven from willow – more like wicker cradles than traditional coffins.

Water has long been associated with death. In many cultures and religions the dead are borne away across a river or sea which separates land of the living from that of the dead. The Etruscans believed that dolphins and seahorses would carry the souls of the dead to the Isles of the Blessed in Elysium. The Greeks depicted Charon ferrying the dead across the Styx. The Aztec paradise was the kingdom of the rain god Tlaloc. Water is also a symbol of the deep, uncharted areas of the psyche. Scientific evidence that all life originally emerged from the ocean seems to explain our instinctive fascination with the sea and the desire of many people for either their bodies or their ashes to be returned to the water rather than the earth. Water is symbolically poured at Buddhist funerals, and used as a ritual cleanser in the rites of many other cultures.

Incense is burned as an offering in many religions, including Buddhist, Christian, Central American and Pagan, to symbolise the ascent of the soul into heaven. In Far Eastern countries sandalwood and sometimes frankincense is used. In the Christian tradition frankincense was brought by one of the Magi from the East as a present for the infant Jesus. In the Book of Revelation (chapter 5, verse 8) St John the Divine alludes to 'golden vials full of odours which are the prayers of the saints'. In Roman Catholic as well as Russian and Greek Orthodox ceremonies it is also burned as a symbol of purification.

Gems and precious metals have always been used in funeral rites because of their indestructibility. Jade, in particular, has associations with immortality. Jade amulets were often buried with the dead, and Chinese emperors were buried in entire suits of jade.

In ancient Egypt lotus wreaths were buried with the dead, who were often buried in rush caskets. In Hindu myth, the world's creator Brahma was born from a lotus blossom growing from the navel of Vishnu, who floated on the primeval lake. In both Hindu and Buddhist religions the lotus is an immensely powerful symbol of spirituality, knowledge and reincarnation. In Europe, white roses have long been associated with death, perhaps because of the Roman festival of Rosalia, a kind of European 'day of the dead', vestiges of which survive today as the *domenica rosata* (rosy Sunday) celebrated on Pentecost Sunday in Italy. For Hindus, marigolds play a large part in the funeral rite, and marigold petals are thrown into the water with the cremated remains. In the West, marigolds are one of the herbs of healing.

White hyacinths symbolise death. In Greek mythology Hyacinthus, a Spartan prince beloved of Apollo and the west wind Zephyrus, was accidentally killed by a discus. The flowers grew from the blood of the dying youth. Violets are often planted on graves, or carved on headstones, and the colour violet is one of the mourning colours. The Greeks associated it with Persephone, who was abducted by Hades as she picked violets, roses and hyacinths in the fields. The Romans celebrated the dead on *dies violaris* (violet day) when they decorated graves with violets.

In the biological sciences, light is literally the life giver. So it is not surprising to find that in the funeral ceremonies of most religions, light and its symbols play a very important role. Light, equated with knowledge and spirituality, is seen as the opposite of darkness, which symbolises ignorance and chaos. Angels and good spirits are manifestations of light, devils and evil spirits thrive in darkness. Candles, bonfires, lamps – sometimes even the sun and the moon themselves – feature in almost all religious rituals. The ancient Egyptian hymn to Akhenaten, the sun king, greeted the life giver with the words 'Beautiful art thou in the brightest spot in heaven, thou living sun, first living thing! Thou art brilliant in the East, and every land hast thou filled with thy beauty.' In neo-paganism the invocation 'drawing down the moon' is an address to the Great Goddess. In Christian texts God 'covered himself with light as with a garment' and Christ declared himself 'the Light of the World'. In the Hindu religion, Krishna is the Lord of Light, and in Islam 'Allah is the light of heaven and earth'. For Buddhists, light symbolises the upward path of the soul towards nirvana.

REMEMBERING THE DEAD

It is a very important part of the mourning process to remember the dead. Even though they are no longer physically there, they live on in the minds of all those who knew them. There are no special occasions for this in British culture. In Mexico there is the Day of the Dead where families take picnics to the graves of dead relatives and dress the plot. In China there is a national day of mourning, where people visit graves, honour their ancestors and remember the dead. In Japan, there is the festival of Tor-Nagashi in mid-August when the dead are remembered by floating lanterns on Lake Matsue with the family name written on one side and a prayer on the other. In Brazil, followers of Macumba do a similar thing on New Year's Eve. Hundreds of thousands of people go to Copacobana beach to propitiate the goddess of the sea. Gifts are put into miniature boats made of card or wood, with a candle in each and the owner's name on the side. At midnight the water is carpeted with white flowers thrown as offerings and the boats with their lighted candles are floated out to sea. A similar ceremony takes place in parts of Asia.

In Britain all we have left is All Hallows' Eve, celebrated on 31 October, which originally had the same purpose, but is now scaled down to Hallowe'en. On All Souls' Day (2 November), generally commemorated in Roman Catholic countries, the veil separating the world of the living and the dead is supposed to be at its thinnest and the souls of the departed are all around us. The largely commercial celebration of Hallowe'en is derived from the traditional belief that evil spirits had to be kept at bay, and prayers said for the souls of the good.

In many cultures, the first anniversary of the death is an important event. It is a good time to hold a public memorial service, or have a small, private ceremony. Take the day off work to visit the grave or the site where the ashes are scattered and place flowers. Light a candle for the dead. Have a feast or celebratory meal. In some places it is traditional to set a place at table for the deceased. Get out the photograph album, listen to your loved one's favourite music. Allow yourself to remember and to grieve.

THE DEATH OF A MUCH-LOVED ANIMAL

This can be a traumatic event both for children and adults. When my beloved cat had to be put to sleep, I cried all the way home from the vet, to the consternation of passers-by and my own embarrassment. It is not sentimental, but perfectly acceptable to grieve for a pet, and it is necessary, both for your own comfort and for public hygiene, to make sure that the body is disposed of in an appropriate way.

If it is a small animal like a hamster, gerbil, goldfish, or even a cat, it may be possible to bury it in a garden. In the case of larger pets, there is always the possibility of future owners of the house digging up the bones. Most vets will arrange for the pet to be cremated for a small charge, and some local authorities will do it free. It is even possible to arrange for mummification, or for the pet to be preserved and stuffed (though taxidermy and embalming are expensive). In some areas there are proper pet cemeteries where animals can be interred.

Some local councils and private cemeteries will allow either the pet or its cremated remains to be interred in a family plot as a 'companion' grave. At a recent ceremony in the north of England, the ashes of the deceased's beloved dog were buried with the body, and the animal was mentioned and commended by the minister conducting the ceremony.

Place the animal in a suitable container – wrap the

body in a towel or a blanket, or place it in a cardboard box. This can then be decorated to your own tastes. The funeral shop Heaven on Earth supplies special caskets for pets, as do the coffin makers E. C. Hodge (MF) Ltd, who are willing to arrange next day delivery (see address list).

Children should be encouraged to say goodbye to their pets, thank them for being their friend, and perhaps include messages or drawings in the shroud. Above all, the animal's body should be treated with respect. This is often a child's first experience of death and it is important that it be sensitively handled. If you believe – as many people do – that the souls of animals survive after death, comfort the child that their pet is in a happier place. If you do not believe in an afterlife, explain that death is part of life and, just as flowers grow, bloom and fade and seed themselves to make new flowers, so animals do the same and the atoms they are composed of become part of other life-forms in nature.

Properly wrapped and mourned, the animal can then be transported to the grave or to the crematorium. There are some excellent animal poems which could be read if you wish, and it is a nice idea for each person to light a candle for the animal and keep it burning until everyone goes to bed. The origin of this custom was to 'light the soul to heaven'. If practicable, plant a small tree or shrub to mark the grave, or place a stone or carved piece of wood. It is not difficult to cut out the pet's name with a stencil and chisel. A small, painted ceramic tile is also fairly easy to make (and fun for children) to be cemented into the wall. A friend recently went to pottery classes to learn how to mould and fire a small model of her dog to place in the garden over its grave. The resulting ceramic statue is a fitting memorial to a much-loved spaniel. Alternatively, you could commission a local artist to do it for you. Many are willing to paint a portrait or sculpt an image from photographs.

Finally, don't replace the pet too soon, before the memory of the old has had time to fade, otherwise the new animal may be resented and disliked.

ANTHOLOGY OF READINGS

VALEDICTION

Give them rest with the devout and the just, in the place of the pasture of rest and of refreshment, of waters in the paradise of delight; whence grief and pain and sighing have fled away.

Early Christian Prayer

To every thing there is a season, and a time to every purpose under the heaven;

A time to be born, and a time to die; a time to plant, and a time to pluck up that which is planted;

A time to hurt, and a time to heal; a time to break down, and a time to build up;

A time to weep, and a time to laugh; a time to mourn, and a time to dance;

A time to cast away stones, and a time to gather
   stones together; a time to embrace, and a time
   to refrain from embracing;
A time to get, and a time to lose; a time to keep
   and a time to cast away;
A time to rend, and a time to sew; a time to keep
   silence and a time to speak;
A time to love and a time to hate; a time of war
   and a time of peace.
To every thing there is a season, and a time to
   every purpose under heaven.

Ecclesiastes, chapter 3, verses 1–8

Death, thy servant, is at my door. He has
   crossed the unknown sea and brought thy call
   to my home.
   The night is dark and my heart is fearful –
   yet I will
   take up the lamp, open my gates and bow to
   him my welcome. It is thy messenger who
   stands at my door.
   I will worship him with folded hands, and
   with tears. I will worship him placing at his
   feet the treasure of my heart.
   He will go back with his errand done, leaving
   a dark shadow on my morning; and in my
   desolate home only my forlorn self will
   remain as my last offering to thee.

Rabindranath Tagore, *Gitanjali*, LXXXVI

QUAKER PRAYER

And this is the Comfort of the Good,
    that the grave cannot hold them,
    and that they live as soon as they die.
    For death is no more
    than a turning of us over from Time to
        Eternity.
    Death, then, being the way and condition of
        Life,
    we cannot love to live,
    if we cannot bear to die.

They that love beyond the World, cannot be
        separated by it,
    Death cannot kill what never dies.
    Nor can Spirits ever be divided
    that love and live in the same Divine Principle,
    the Root and Record of their Friendship.
    If Absence be not death, neither is theirs.

Death is but Crossing the World, as Friends do
    the Seas.

William Penn

DO NOT STAND AT MY GRAVE

Do not stand at my grave and weep;
I am not there. I do not sleep.

I am a thousand winds that blow.
I am the diamond glints on the snow.
I am the gentle autumn's rain.
When you awaken in the morning's hush,
I am the swift uplifting rush
Of quiet birds in circled flight.
I am the soft stars that shine at night.
Do not stand at my grave and cry;
I am not there. I did not die.

Anon (possibly North American Indian prayer)

The Lord had anointed me to preach good tidings
    unto the meek;
he hath sent me to bind up the brokenhearted,
to proclaim liberty to the captives,
and the opening of the prison to them that are
    bound;
to comfort all that mourn
to give unto them beauty for ashes,
the oil of joy for mourning,
the garment of praise for the spirit of heaviness . . .

For the mountains shall depart
and the hills be removed
but my kindness shall not depart from thee
neither shall the covenant of my peace be
    removed, Saith the Lord.

Isaiah, chapter 61, verses 1–4; chapter 54, verse
    10

WHEN I AM DEAD

When I am dead
Cry for me a little
Think of me sometimes
But not too much.
Think of me now and again
As I was in life
At some moments it's pleasant to recall
But not for long.
Leave me in peace
And I shall leave you in peace
And while you live
Let your thoughts be with the living.

Anon (traditional Indian prayer)

THE BURNING OF LEAVES

Now is the time for the burning of leaves.
They go to the fire; the nostril pricks with
    smoke
Wandering slowly into a weeping mist.
Brittle and blotched, ragged and rotten sheaves!
A flame seizes the smouldering ruin and bites
On stubborn stalks that crackle as they resist.

The last hollyhock's fallen tower is dust:
All the spices of June are a bitter reek,
All the extravagant riches spent and mean.
All burns! The reddest rose is a ghost;
Sparks whirl up, to expire in the mist: the wild
Fingers of fire are making corruption clean.

Now is the time for stripping the spirit bare,
Time for the burning of days ended and done,
Idle solace of things that have gone before,
Rootless hope and fruitless desire are there:
Let them go to the fire with never a look
    behind.
The world that was ours is a world that is ours
    no more.

They will come again, the leaf and the flower, to
    arise
From squalor of rottenness into the old
    splendour,
And magical scents to a wondering memory
    bring:
The same glory, to shine upon different eyes.
Earth cares for her own ruins, naught for ours.
Nothing is certain, only the certain spring.

Laurence Binyon

THE FRONTIER

Now. When I have overcome my fears – of
    others, of myself, of the underlying darkness:
at the frontier of the unheard-of.
Here ends the known. But from a source
    beyond it,
something fills my being with its possibilities –
At the frontier.

Dag Hammarskjöld, *Markings*

FAREWELL

Farewell to Thee! But not farewell
To all my fondest thoughts of Thee;
Within my heart they still shall dwell
And they shall cheer and comfort me.

Life seems more sweet that Thou didst live
And men more true that Thou wert one;
Nothing is lost that Thou didst give,
Nothing destroyed that Thou hast done.

Anne Brontë

LAMENT

Once, ritual lament would have been chanted:
women would have been paid to beat their
    breasts
and howl for you all night, when all is silent.
Where can we find such customs now? So many
have long since disappeared or been disowned.
That's what you have come for; to retrieve
the laments that were omitted. Can you hear
    me?
I would like to fling out my voice like a cloth
over the fragments of your death, and keep
pulling at it until it is torn to pieces,
and all my words would have to walk around
shivering, in the tatters of that voice;
if lament were enough.

Rainer Maria Rilke

FAREWELL

A little while and
I will be gone from among you,
whither I cannot tell.
From nowhere we come;
into nowhere we go.

What is life?
It is the flash of a firefly
in the night.
It is a breath of a buffalo
in the winter time.
It is the little shadow
that runs across the grass
and loses itself in the sunset.

Chief Crowfoot

No man is an island, entire of itself; every man is a
piece of the continent, a part of the main; if a clod
be washed away by the sea, Europe is the less, as
well as if a promontory were, as well as if a manor
of thy friends or of thine own were; any man's death
diminishes me, because I am involved in Mankind;
and therefore never send to know for whom the bell
tolls; it tolls for thee.

John Donne, *Devotions*, Meditation XVII

ETERNAL LOVE

Leave me, O love, which reachest but to dust,
    And thou, my mind, aspire to higher things!
Grow rich in that which never taketh rust:
    Whatever fades, but fading pleasure brings.

Draw in thy beams, and humble all thy might
  To that sweet yoke where lasting freedoms
    be;
Which breaks the clouds and opens forth the
  light
  That doth both shine and give us sight to see.
O take fast hold! let that light be thy guide
  In this small course which birth draws out to
    death,
And think how evil becometh him to slide
  Who seeketh Heaven, and comes of heavenly
  breath.
    Then farewell, world! thy uttermost I see:
    Eternal Love, maintain thy life in me!

Sir Philip Sidney

NO COWARD SOUL

No Coward soul is mine,
No trembler in the world's storm-troubled
  sphere;
I see Heaven's glories shine
And Faith shines equal arming me from Fear.

O God within my breast,
Almighty ever-present Deity
Life, that in me hast rest
As I, Undying Life, have power in Thee.

Vain are the thousand creeds
That move men's hearts, unutterably vain,
Worthless as withered weeds
Or idlest froth amid the boundless main

To waken doubt in one
Holding so fast by thy infinity,
So surely anchored on
The steadfast rock of Immortality.

With wide-embracing love
Thy spirit animates eternal years,
Pervades and broods above,
Changes, sustains, dissolves, creates and rears.

Though Earth and moon were gone
And suns and universes ceased to be
And thou wert left alone
Every Existence would exist in thee.

There is not room for Death
Nor atom that his might could render void
Since thou art Being and Breath
And what thou art may never be destroyed.

Emily Brontë

For since by man came death, by man came also
the resurrection of the dead.

For as in Adam all die, even so in Christ shall all
be made alive.

But every man in his own order: Christ the
firstfruits; afterward they that are Christ's at
his coming.

Then cometh the end, when he shall have
delivered up the kingdom to God, even the
Father; when he shall have put down all rule
and all authority and power;

For he must reign, till he hath put all enemies
under his feet.

The last enemy that shall be destroyed is death.

I Corinthians, chapter 15, verses 21–6

Death is a clean bold word and has no second
meaning.

Death means an end. By sight, touch, temperature
we know.

Do not insult this strong word with a weak evasion

And say, 'He has gone on' – 'He passed away' –
'He sleeps'.

Speak not of the body and its lively grace

As paltry things that never mattered after all,

Creative hands and giving hands, hands calloused
and deformed.

As being nothing now but broken tools.

If you believe the soul, denied the dear familiar
    flesh
Finds other place to live, keep to your faith,
But grant the body it illumined your candid grief.

Or, if you must believe that when the light went
    out
Of eyes you loved and they stared back and told
    you nothing,
For that was all that could be told forever,
Salute Death. He demands you shall attain

Your fullest strength of honesty and courage.
You shall not bear your sorrow's weight upon a
    crutch of words,
You will stand straight, nor say your lover, friend,
    your child
Has 'gone' as though he'd wandered off somewhere,
But speak with dignity and say 'He died'.

Rebecca Richmond

Lord, without our consent we are born, without our
consent we live, without our consent we die, without
our consent our bodies return to the grave and our
spirit goes forward to life everlasting. We cannot
always understand Your plans and we do not see Your
ways, for our minds are overwhelmed and our eyes are
too weak. Yet to comfort us and give us hope You lift
the veil of eternity, and we are permitted to know that

the world is a corridor, and we are on a journey, that the end is perfection, and the reward is peace.

For a short time You gave into our care a child whom we loved. Our hearts would be broken if we did not know that You are love itself, which makes good all that is lost. The tears would never leave our eyes, if we did not know that at the end You bring all together, with mercy and tenderness, in the gathering of life. Therefore with sadness and with hope we commend the soul of [name] into your care. You are with her/him, we cannot fear.

from the Jewish Funeral Service

TROPICAL DEATH

The fat black woman want
a brilliant tropical death
not a cold sojourn
in some North Europe far/forlorn

The fat black woman want
some heat/hibiscus at her feet
blue sea dress
to wrap her neat

The fat black woman want
some bawl
no quiet jerk tear wiping
a polite hearse withdrawal

The fat black woman want
all her dead rights
first night
third night
nine night
all the sleepless droning
red-eyed wake nights

In the heart
of her mother's sweetbreast
of the sun leaf's cool bless
In the bloom
of her people's bloodrest

the fat black woman want
a brilliant tropical death yes.

Grace Nichols

THE SECRET OF DEATH

Then Almitra spoke, saying, We would ask now
    of Death.
And he said:
You would know the secret of death.
But how shall you find it unless you seek it in
    the heart of life?
The owl whose night-bound eyes are blind unto
    the day cannot unveil the mystery of light.

If you would indeed behold the spirit of death,
open your heart unto the body of life.
For life and death are one, even as the river and
the sea are one.

In the depth of your hopes and desires lies your
silent knowledge of the beyond;
And, like seeds dreaming beneath the snow your
heart dreams of spring.
Trust the dreams, for in them is hidden the gate
to eternity.
Your fear of death is but the trembling of the
shepherd when he stands before the king
whose hand is to be laid upon him in honour.
Is the shepherd not joyful beneath his
trembling, that he shall wear the mark of the
king?
Yet is he not more mindful of his trembling?

For what is it to die but to stand naked in the
wind and to melt into the sun?
And what is it to cease breathing but to free the
breath from its restless tides, that it may rise
and expand and seek God unencumbered?

Only when you drink from the river of silence
shall you indeed sing.
And when you have reached the mountain top,
then you shall begin to climb.

And when the earth shall claim your limbs, then
   shall you truly dance.

Kahlil Gibran, *The Prophet*

IF I SHOULD DIE

(read at the funeral of Diana, Princess of Wales,
Westminster Abbey, September 1997)

If I should die and leave you here awhile,
Be not like others, sore undone, who keep
Long vigils by the silent dust and weep.
For my sake turn again to life and smile,
Nerving thy heart and trembling hand to do
Something to comfort other hearts than thine.
Complete those dear unfinished tasks of mine
And I, perchance, may therein comfort you.

Variously attributed to: Thomas Gray, anon and
   A. Price Hughes

POSTSCRIPT: FOR GWENO

If I should go away,
Beloved, do not say
'He has forgotten me'.
For you abide,
A singing rib within my dreaming side;

You always stay.
And in the mad tormented valley
Where blood and hunger rally
And Death the wild beast is uncaught, untamed,
Our soul withstands the terror
And has its quiet honour
Among the glittering stars your voices named.

Alun Lewis

LOVE

Though I speak with the tongues of men and of angels, and have not Love I am become as sounding brass, or a tinkling cymbal. And though I have the gift of prophecy and understand all mysteries and all knowledge; and though I have faith, so that I could remove mountains and have not Love I am nothing, and though I bestow all my goods to feed the poor and though I give my body to be burned and have not Love it profiteth me nothing.

Love suffereth long and is kind; Love envieth not; Love vaunteth not itself, is not puffed up; doth not behave itself unseemly, seeketh not her own, is not easily provoked, thinketh no evil; rejoiceth not in iniquity, but rejoiceth in the truth; beareth all things, believeth all things, hopeth all things, endureth all things.

Love never faileth; but whether there be prophe-
cies, they shall fail; whether there be tongues,
they shall cease; whether there be knowledge,
it shall vanish away. For we know imperfectly
and we prophesy imperfectly. But when that
which is perfect is come, then that which is
imperfect shall be done away.

When I was a child, I spake as a child, I understood as a child, I thought as a child; but when
I became a man, I put away childish things.
For now we see through glass, darkly, but then
face to face; now I know imperfectly, but then
I shall I know even as also I am known. And
now abideth Faith, Hope and Love – these
three; but the greatest of these is Love.

I Corinthians, chapter 13, verses 1–13

THE CURFEW TOLLS

The curfew tolls the knell of parting day,
The lowing herd winds slowly o'er the lea,
The ploughman homeward plods his weary way,
And leaves the world to darkness, and to me.

Now fades the glimmering landscape on the
sight,
And all the air a solemn stillness holds;

Save where the beetle wheels his droning flight,
And drowsy tinklings lull the distant folds.

Beneath those rugged elms, that yew-tree's
    shade,
Where heaves the turf in many a mouldering
    heap,
Each in his narrow cell for ever laid,
The rude forefathers of the hamlet sleep.

The breezy call of incense-breathing morn,
The swallow twittering from the straw-built
    shed,
The cock's shrill clarion, or the echoing horn,
No more shall rouse them from their lowly bed.

For them no more the blazing hearth shall burn,
Or busy housewife ply her evening care;
No children run to lisp their sire's return,
Or climb his knees the envied kiss to share.

Oft did the harvest to their sickle yield,
Their furrow oft the stubborn glebe has broke;
How jocund did they drive their team afield!
How bowed the woods beneath their sturdy
    stroke!

Let not ambition mock their useful toil,
Their homely joys and destiny obscure;

Nor grandeur hear with a disdainful smile,
The short and simple annals of the poor.

The boast of heraldry, the pomp of power,
And all that beauty, all that wealth e'er gave,
Awaits alike the inevitable hour.
The paths of glory lead but to the grave.

Thomas Gray, from *Elegy Written in a Country Churchyard*

PRAYER OF ST DENIS

You are wisdom, uncreated and eternal,
    the supreme First Cause, above all being,
    sovereign Godhead, sovereign goodness,
    watching unseen the God-inspired wisdom of
    Christian people.
Raise us, we pray, that we may totally respond
    to the supreme, unknown, ultimate, and
    splendid height
    of your words, mysterious and inspired.
There all God's secret matters lie covered and
    hidden
    under darkness both profound and brilliant,
    silent and wise.
You make what is ultimate and beyond
    brightness
    secretly to shine in all that is most dark.

In your way, ever unseen and intangible,
you fill to the full with most beautiful
splendour
those souls who close their eyes that they may
see.
And I, please, with love that goes on beyond
mind
to all that is beyond mind,
seek to gain such for myself through this
prayer.

Anon, *The Cloud of Unknowing* (fourteenth
century)

Remember now thy creator in the days of thy
youth, while the evil days come not, nor the
years draw nigh, when thou shalt say, I have
no pleasure in them;
While the sun, or the light, or the moon, or the
stars, be not darkened, nor the clouds return
after the rain;
In the day when the keepers of the house shall
tremble, and the strong men shall bow themselves, and the grinders cease because they are
few, and those that look out of the windows be
darkened.
And the doors shall be shut in the streets, when
the sound of the grinding is low, and he shall
rise up at the voice of the bird, and all the
daughters of music shall be brought low;

Also when they shall be afraid of that which is
  high, and fears shall be in the way, and the
  almond tree shall flourish, and the grasshopper
  shall be a burden, and desire shall fail; because
  man goeth to his long home, and the mourners
  go about the streets.
Or ever the silver cord be loosed, or the golden
  bowl be broken, or the pitcher be broken at the
  fountain, or the wheel broken at the cistern.
Then shall the dust return to the earth as it was:
  and the spirit shall return unto God who gave
  it.

Ecclesiastes, chapter 12, verses 1–7

TIME AND GRIEF

O time! who know'st a lenient hand to lay
Softest on sorrow's wound, and slowly thence
(Lulling to sad repose the weary sense)
    The faint pang stealest unperceived away;
    On thee I rest my only hope at last,
And think, when thou has dried the bitter tear
That flows in vain o'er all my soul held dear,
    I may look back on every sorrow past,
    And meet life's peaceful evening with a smile:
As some long bird, at day's departing hour,
Sings in the sunbeam, of the transient shower

Forgetful, though its wings are wet the while:–
Yet ah! how much must this poor heart endure,
Which hopes from thee, and thee alone, a cure!

William Lisle Bowles

BELIEF

I have to believe
That you still exist
Somewhere,
That you still watch me
Sometimes,
That you still love me
Somehow.

I have to believe
That life has meaning
Somehow,
That I am useful here
Sometimes,
That I make small differences
Somewhere.

I have to believe
That I need to stay here
For some time,
That all this teaches me
Something,

So that I can meet you again
Somewhere.

Ann Thorp

THE DESIRE TO BECOME ONE WITH THE UNIVERSE

Having drunk deeply of the heaven above and felt
the most glorious beauty of the day, I desire now to
become lost and absorbed into the being or existence
of the universe. Deep into the earth under, and high
above into the sky, and further still to the sun and
stars, still further beyond the stars into the hollow
of space, losing thus my separateness of being to
become a part of the whole.

With the glory of the great sea, I pray; with the
firm, solid, and sustaining earth; the depth, distance,
and the expanse of ether; the age, tamelessness, and
ceaseless motion of the ocean; the stars, and the
unknown in space, by all those things which are most
powerful known to me, I pray. Not in words, my
soul prays that I may have something from each of
these, that I may have in myself the secret and meaning of the earth, the golden sun, the light, the foam-
flecked sea. Let my soul become enlarged; I am not
enough; I am little and contemptible. I desire a great-
ness of soul, an irradiance of mind, a deeper insight,
a broader hope.

Richard Jeffries, from *The Story of my Heart*

A SONG OF LIVING

Because I have loved life, I shall have no sorrow
   to die.
I have sent up my gladness on wings, to be lost
   in the blue of the sky.
I have run and leaped with the rain, I have
   taken the wind to my breast.
My cheek like a drowsy child to the face of the
   earth I have pressed.
Because I have loved life, I shall have no sorrow
   to die.

I have kissed young Love on the lips, I have
   heard his song to the end.
I have struck my hand like a seal in the loyal
   hand of a friend.
I have known the peace of heaven, the comfort
   of work done well.
I have longed for death in the darkness and
   risen alive out of hell.
Because I have loved life, I shall have no sorrow
   to die.

I give a share of my soul to the world where my
   course is run.
I know that another shall finish the task I must
   leave undone.

I know that no flower, nor flint was in vain on
the path I trod.
As one looks on a face through a window,
through life I have looked on God.
Because I have loved life, I shall have no sorrow
to die.

Amelia Josephine Burr

DEATH BE NOT PROUD

Death be not proud, though some have called
thee
Mighty and dreadful, for thou art not so,
For, those, whom thou think'st thou dost
overthrow,
Die not, poor death, nor yet canst thou kill me;
From rest and sleep, which but thy pictures be,
Much pleasure, then from thee, much more
must flow,
And soonest our best men with thee do go,
Rest of their bones, and soul's delivery.
Thou art slave to Fate, Chance, kings, and
desperate men,
And dost with poison, war, and sickness dwell,
And poppy, or charms can make us sleep as
well,
And better than thy stroke; why swell'st thou
then?

One short sleep past, we wake eternally,
And death shall be no more; death, thou shalt
    die!

John Donne, *Holy Sonnets*, x

Death meets us everywhere, and is procured by every instrument, and in all chances, and enters in at many doors, by violence and secret influence, by the aspect of a star and the stench of a mist, by the emissions of a cloud and the meeting of a vapour, by the fall of a chariot and the stumbling at a stone, by a full meal or an empty stomach, by watching at the wine or by watching at prayers; by the sun or the moon; by a heat or a cold; by sleepless nights or sleeping days; by water frozen into the hardness and sharpness of a dagger, or water thawed into the floods of a river; by a hair or a raisin; by violent motion or sitting still; by severity or dissolution; by God's mercy or God's anger; by everything in Providence and everything in manners; by everything in nature and everything in chance.

Let no man extend his thoughts, or let his hopes wander towards future and far-distant events and accidental contingencies. This day is mine and yours, but ye know not what shall be on the morrow; and every morning creeps out of a dark cloud, leaving behind it an ignorance and silence deep as midnight, so that we cannot discern what comes hereafter, unless we had a light from heaven brighter than the vision of an angel, even in the spirit of prophecy.

Jeremy Taylor, *Holy Dying*

FOUND LINES

(Sir Walter Raleigh to his wife 1603)

Dear Bess, I would not send you grief,
though I am no more yours, you mine.
Bear this with good heart, like thy self.

Long mourning's vain – again be wife,
since this thy husband's overthrown.
Dear Bess, I would not send you grief.

Almighty God, goodness itself,
keep thee; repose yourself in him.
Bear this with good heart, like thy self.

But for your sake I sued for life,
and for our boy's, a true man's son.
Dear Bess, I would not send you grief –

nor want, being thus surprised with death
and unresolved each debt and loan.
bear this with good heart. Like thyself

while others sleep I watch, time's thief.
Yours that was, but not now my own,
dear Bess. I would not send you grief –
bear this with good heart, like thy self.

Pamela Gillilan

PSALM 121

I will lift up mine eyes unto the hills, from whence
  cometh my help.
My help cometh even from the Lord, who hath
  made heaven and earth.
He will not suffer thy foot to be moved, and he
  that keepeth thee will not sleep.
Behold, he that keepeth Israel, shall neither slumber nor sleep.
The Lord himself is thy keeper, the Lord is thy
  defence upon thy right hand.
So that the sun shall not burn thee by day, neither
  the moon by night.
The Lord shall preserve thee from all evil, yea, it
  is even he that shall keep thy soul.
The Lord shall preserve thy going out and thy
  coming in, from this time forth for evermore.

SLEEPING AT LAST

Sleeping at last, the trouble and tumult over,
  Sleeping at last, the struggle and horror
  past,
Cold and white, out of sight of friend and of
  lover,
  Sleeping at last.

No more a tired heart downcast or overcast,
  No more pangs that wring or shifting fears
  that hover,
Sleeping at last in a dreamless sleep locked fast.

Fast asleep. Singing birds in their leafy cover
  Cannot wake her, nor shake her the gusty
  blast.
Under the purple thyme and the purple clover
  Sleeping at last.

Christina Rossetti

I have got my leave. Bid me farewell, my brothers!
I bow to you all and take my departure.

Here I give back the keys of my door – and I give
up all claims to my house. I only ask for last kind
words from you.

We were neighbours for long, but I received more
than I could give. Now the day has dawned and the

lamp that lit my dark corner is out. A summons has come and I am ready for my journey.

Rabindranath Tagore, *Gitanjali*, XCIII

REFLECTIONS ON ETERNITY

It is eternity now. I am in the midst of it. It is about me in the sunshine; I am in it, as the butterfly floats in the light-laden air. Nothing has to come; it is now. Now is eternity; now is the immortal life. Here this moment, on earth now; I exist in it. The years, the centuries, the cycles are absolutely nothing. To the soul there is no past and no future; all is and will be ever, in now. Haste not, be at rest, this Now is eternity.

Richard Jeffries, from *The Story of my Heart*

'I came like Water, and like Wind I go'.

Into this Universe, and *why* not knowing,
Nor *whence*, like Water willy-nilly flowing!
And out of it, as Wind along the Waste,
I know not *whither*, willy-nilly blowing.

Alas, that Spring should vanish with the Rose!
That Youth's sweet-scented Manuscript should
    close!

The Nightingale that in the Branches sang,
Ah, whence, and whither flown again, who
knows?

There was a Door to which I found no Key;
There was a Veil past which I could not see;
Some little talk awhile of Me and Thee
There seemed – and then no more of Thee and
Me.

One Moment in annihilation's waste,
One Moment of the Well of Life to taste –
The Stars are setting and the Caravan
Starts for the Dawn of Nothing – Oh, make
haste!

And if the Wine you drink, the Lip you Press,
End in the Nothing all Things end in – Yes –
Then fancy while Thou art, Thou art but what
Thou shalt be – Nothing – Thou shalt not be
less.

I sometimes think that never blows so red
The Rose as where some buried Caesar bled
That every Hyacinth the Garden wears
Dropt in its Lap from some once lovely Head.

And this delightful Herb whose tender Green
Fledges the River's Lip on which we lean –
Ah, lean upon it lightly! for who knows

From what once Lovely Lip it springs unseen!

Ah Moon of my Delight who know'st no Wane,
The Moon of Heaven is rising once again:
How oft hereafter rising shall she look
Through this same Garden after me – in vain!

And when Thyself with shining Foot shall pass
Among the Guests Star-scattered on the Grass
And in thy joyous Errand reach the Spot
Where I made one – turn down an empty Glass!

from *The Rubáiyát of Omar Khayyám,*
translated by Edward FitzGerald

CROSSING THE BRIDGE AT DEATH

We gather here to say farewell to a friend who must
travel far. There is a reason for being here in this
world and this life. There is a reason for leaving
when the purposes of this life are done. The soul
must journey beyond to pause, to rest, to wait for
those who are loved. For the world beyond is a land
of eternal summer and of joy, far from the cares of
this world, with happiness and youth anew.
*[Three evergreen branches are placed on top of the
coffin.]*
As the evergreen does grow and prosper both in summer and in winter, year after year, so also does the

soul continue from life to life, growing ever stronger, wiser and richer.

Wiccan Rites

AND DEATH SHALL HAVE NO DOMINION

And death shall have no dominion.
Dead men naked they shall be one
With the man in the wind and the west moon;
When their bones are picked clean and the clean
    bones gone,
They shall have stars at elbow and foot;
Though they go mad they shall be sane,
Though they sink through the sea they shall rise
    again;
Though lovers be lost, love shall not;
And death shall have no dominion.

And death shall have no dominion.
Under the windings of the sea
They lying long shall not die windily;
Twisting on racks when sinews give way,
Strapped to a wheel, yet they shall not break;
Faith in their hands shall snap in two,
And the unicorn evils run them through;
Split all ends up they shan't crack;
And death shall have no dominion.

And death shall have no dominion.
No more may gulls cry at their ears
Or waves break loud on the seashores;
Where blew a flower may a flower no more
Lift its head to the blows of the rain;
Though they be made and dead as nails,
Heads of the characters hammer through
    daisies;
Break in the sun till the sun breaks down,
And death shall have no dominion.

Dylan Thomas

REQUIEM

Under the wide and starry sky,
Dig the grave and let me lie.
Glad did I live and gladly die,
    And I laid me down with a will.
This be the verse you grave for me:
'Here he lies where he longed to be;
Home is the sailor, home from the sea,
    And the hunter home from the hill.'

R. L. Stevenson

REMEMBER

Remember me when I am gone away,
Gone far away into the silent land;
  When you can no more hold me by the hand,
  Nor I half turn to go, yet turning stay.
Remember me when no more day by day
You tell me of our future that you plann'd:
  Only remember me; you understand
  It will be late to counsel then or pray.
Yet if you should forget me for a while
And afterwards remember, do not grieve:
  For if the darkness and corruption leave
  A vestige of the thoughts that once I had,
Better by far you should forget and smile
Than that you should remember and be sad.

Christina Rossetti

PSALM 23

The Lord is my shepherd, I shall not want.
He shall feed me in a green pasture, and lead me
    forth beside the waters of comfort.
He shall convert my soul, and bring me forth in
    the paths of righteousness, for his name's sake.
Yea, though I walk through the valley of the

shadow of death, I will fear no evil, for thou art with me; thy rod and thy staff comfort me.

Thou shalt prepare a table before me against them that trouble me, thou hast anointed my head with oil, and my cup runneth over.

But thy loving-kindness and mercy shall follow me all the days of my life, and I will dwell in the house of the Lord for ever.

IN THE HOPE OF ETERNAL LIFE

Let not your heart be troubled, you believe in God, believe also in me. In my Father's house are many mansions; if it were not so, I would have told you. I go to prepare a place for you. And if I go and prepare a place for you I will come again, and receive you unto myself; that where I am, you may be also. And where I go you know and the way you know.

Peace I leave with you, my peace I give unto you; not as the world giveth, give I unto you. Let not your heart be troubled, neither let it be afraid.

St John, chapter 14, verses 1–3 and 27

I am the resurrection and the life, saith the Lord. He that believeth in me, though he were dead, yet shall he live, and whosoever liveth and believeth in me shall never die.

St John, chapter 11, verses 25–6

I know that my Redeemer liveth, and that he shall stand at the latter day upon the earth. And though after my skin worms destroy this body, yet in my flesh shall I see God, whom I shall see for myself and mine eyes shall behold and not another.

Job, chapter 19, verses 25–7

But some man will say 'How are the dead raised up: and with what body do they come?' Thou fool, that which thou sowest is not quickened, except it die. And that which thou sowest, thou sowest not the body that shall be, but bare grain, it may chance of wheat or of some other grain, but God giveth it a body and to every seed his own body.

All flesh is not the same flesh; but there is one kind of flesh of men, another flesh of beasts, another of fishes, and another of birds. There are also celestial bodies, and bodies terrestrial. But the glory of the celestial is one, and the glory of the terrestrial is another. There is one glory of the sun and another glory of the moon and another glory of the stars, for one star differeth from another star in glory.

So also is the resurrection of the dead. It is sown in corruption, it is raised in incorruption. It is sown in dishonour, it is raised in glory. It is sown in weakness, it is raised in power. It is sown a natural body, it is raised a spiritual body. There is a natural body and there is a spiritual body. . . . And as we have borne the image of the earthy, we shall also bear the image of the heavenly. . . .

Behold, I show you a mystery. We shall not all sleep but we shall all be changed, in a moment, in the twinkling of an eye, at the last trump, when the trumpet shall sound and the dead shall be raised incorruptible and we shall be changed. . . . Then shall be brought to pass the saying that is written: Death is swallowed up in victory. O Death, where is thy sting? O Grave, where is thy victory?

I Corinthians, chapter 15, verses 35–55

We do not see them go
From visible into invisible like gossamer in the
    sun.
Bodies by spirit raised

Fall as dust to dust when the wind drops,
Moth-wing and chrysalis.
Those who live us and outlive us do not stay,
But leave empty their semblances, icons, bodies
Of long-enduring gold, or the fleet golden
    flower
On which the Buddha smiled.
In vain we look for them where others found
    them,
For by the vanishing stair of time immortals are
    for ever departing;
But while we gaze after the receding vision
Others are already descending through gates of
    ivory and horn.

Kathleen Raine, from *Scala coeli*

BLACKBIRD

Blackbird singing in the dead of night
Take these broken wings and learn to fly.
All your life
You were only waiting for this moment to arise.
Blackbird singing in the dead of night
Take these sunken eyes and learn to see.
All your life
You were only waiting for this moment to be
    free.
Blackbird fly, Blackbird fly

Into the light of the dark black night.
Blackbird fly, Blackbird fly
Into the light of the dark black night
Blackbird singing in the dead of night
Take these broken wings and learn to fly.
All your life
You were only waiting for this moment to arise
You were only waiting for this moment to arise
You were only waiting for this moment to arise.

John Lennon and Paul McCartney

THE STORY OF KISA GOTAMI

Kisa Gotami's first baby fell ill and died before it was a year old. Grief-stricken and unable to accept the death, she carried the dead child from house to house asking for help to find someone to cure him. Everywhere she was laughed at and ridiculed. Eventually someone directed her to the Great Healer. He listened to her petition and agreed to help her. 'The only thing that will heal your child', he said, 'is a pinch of mustard seed from the house of a family where no one has ever died.'

Kisa Gotami gladly went away to begin her search. She went from house to house, from village to village, but nowhere could she find a family where none had died.

When she went back to the Great Healer, he told her gently, 'Did you imagine that you alone had lost someone you greatly loved? All living things are subject to one unchanging law – the Prince of Death, who like a raging torrent bears all things towards the sea.'

'Teach me the truth,' Kisa Gotami said. 'Teach me what is beyond death, and what there is within me that will not die.'

'There is only one way out of the ocean of unbearable suffering, of the endless cycle of birth and death', answered the Buddha. 'Pain has made you learn, and to follow the path to liberation through enlightenment which I will now show you.'

Then Kisa Gotami entered upon the first stage of her spiritual journey towards Nirvana. She meditated on the oil lamps, flickering and flaring in the temple. 'Even as it is with these flames, so also it is with living beings here in the world', she thought. 'Some flare up and are born, while others flicker and die. Only those that have reached Nirvana are quenched.'

Traditional (fuller version in *The Tibetan Book of the Dead*)

THOUGHTS ON LIFE, DEATH AND REBIRTH

The books say well, my Brothers! each man's life
The outcome of his former living is;
The bygone wrongs bring forth sorrows and
    woes,
The bygone right breeds bliss.

That which ye sow, ye reap. See yonder fields!
The sesamun was sesamun, the corn was corn.
    The Silence and the darkness knew!
So is man's fate born.

If he shall labour rightly, rooting these,
And planting wholesome seedlings where they
    grew,
Fruitful and fair and clean the ground shall be
And rich the harvest due.

Buddhist Funeral Ceremony

FEAR NO MORE

Fear no more the heat of the sun,
    Nor the furious winter's rages;
Thou thy worldly task hast done,
    Home art gone, and ta'en thy wages;

Golden lads and girls all must,
As chimney-sweepers come to dust.

Fear no more the frown of the great,
    Thou art past the tyrant's stroke;
Care no more to clothe and eat,
    To thee the reed is as the oak;
The sceptre, learning, physic, must
All follow this and come to dust.

Fear no more the lightning flash,
    Nor the all-dreaded thunder-stone;
Fear not slander, censure rash,
    Thou hast finished joy and moan;
All lovers young, all lovers must
Consign to thee and come to dust.

No exorciser harm thee!
Nor no witchcraft charm thee!
Ghost unlaid forbear thee!
Nothing ill come near thee!
Quiet consummation have;
And renowned be thy grave!

William Shakespeare, *Cymbeline*, Act IV, scene 2

Death is nothing at all. . . . I have only slipped away
into the next room. I am I and you are you. Whatever
we were to each other that we are still. Call me by
my old familiar name, speak to me in the easy way

which you always used. Put no difference in your tone; wear no enforced air of solemnity or sorrow. Laugh as we always laughed at the little jokes we enjoyed together. Play, smile, think of me, pray for me. Let my name be ever the household word that it always was. Let it be spoken without effort, without the ghost of a shadow on it. Life means all that it ever meant. It is the same as it ever was; there is absolutely unbroken continuity. Why should I be out of mind because I am out of sight? I am waiting for you for an interval, somewhere very near, just around the corner. All is well.

Henry Scott Holland, Death is Nothing at All, from *Facts of the Faith*

PRAYER OF ST FRANCIS OF ASSISI

Lord make me an instrument of Thy peace.
Where there is hatred, let me sow love;
Where there is injury, pardon;
Where there is doubt, faith;
Where there is despair, hope;
Where there is darkness, light;
Where there is sadness, joy.

O Divine Master, grant that
I may not so much seek
To be consoled, as to console;

Not so much to be understood as
To understand; not so much to be
Loved as to love:

For it is in giving that we receive;
It is in pardoning, that we are pardoned;
It is in dying, that we awaken to eternal life.

He has outsoared the shadow of our night;
Envy and calumny, and hate and pain,
And that unrest which men miscall delight,
Can touch him not and torture not again;
From the contagion of the world's slow stain
He is secure, and now can never mourn
A heart grown cold, and head grown grey in
 vain;
Nor, when the spirit's self has ceased to burn,
With sparkless ashes load an unlamented urn.

He is made one with Nature: there is heard
His voice in all her music, from the moan
Of thunder, to the song of night's sweet bird;
He is a presence to be felt and known
In darkness and in light, from herb and stone,
Spreading itself where'er that Power may move
Which has withdrawn his being to its own; . . .

He is a portion of the loveliness
Which once he made more lovely: . . .

And bursting in its beauty and its might
From trees and beasts and men into the
Heaven's light.

Percy Bysshe Shelley, *Adonais*, XL–XLIII

I THANK THEE

I thank Thee, God, that I have lived
In this great world and known its many joys;
The song of birds, the strong, sweet scent of
hay
And cooling breezes in the secret dusk,
The flaming sunsets at the close of day,
Hills, and the lonely, heather-covered moors,
Music at night, and moonlight on the sea,
The beat of waves upon the rocky shore
And wild, white spray, flung high in ecstasy:
The faithful eyes of dogs, and treasured books.
The love of kin and fellowship of friends,
And all that makes life dear and beautiful.
I thank Thee, too, that there has come to me
A little sorrow and, sometimes, defeat,
A little heartache and the loneliness
That comes with parting, and the word,
'Goodbye',
Dawn breaking after dreary hours of pain,
When I discovered that night's gloom *must* yield
And morning light break through to me again.

Because of these and other blessings poured
Unasked upon my wondering head,
Because I know that there is yet to come
An even richer and more glorious life,
And most of all, because Thine only Son
Once sacrificed life's loveliness for me –
I thank Thee, God, that I have lived.

Elizabeth Craven

SETTING SAIL

Exultation is the going
Of an inland soul to sea,
Past the houses – past the headlands –
Into deep Eternity –

Bred as we, among the mountains,
Can the sailor understand
The divine intoxication
Of the first league out from land.

Emily Dickinson

IF IT MUST BE

If it must be
You speak no more with us,
Nor smile no more with us,

Nor walk no more with us,
Then let us take a patience and a calm.
For even now the green leaf explodes,
Sun lightens stone and all the river burns.

Anon

OH EARTH, WAIT FOR ME

Return me, oh sun,
to my wild destiny,
rain of the ancient wood,
bring me back the aroma and the swords
that fall from the sky,
the solitary peace of pasture and rock,
the damp at the river-margins,
the smell of the larch tree,
the wind alive like a heart
beating in the crowded restlessness
of the towering araucaria.

Earth, give me back your pure gifts,
the towers of silence which rose
from the solemnity of their roots.
I want to go back to being what I have not
    been,
and learn to go back from such deeps
that amongst all natural things
I could live or not live; it does not matter

to be one stone more, the dark stone,
the pure stone which the river bears away.

Pablo Neruda

FROM TOO MUCH LOVE OF LIVING

From too much love of living,
From hope and fear set free,
We thank with brief thanksgiving,
Whatever gods may be
That no life lives for ever;
That dead men rise up never;
That even the weariest river
Winds somewhere safe to sea.

Then star nor sun shall waken,
Nor any change of light;
Nor sound or waters shaken,
Nor any sound or sight;
Nor wintry leaves nor vernal,
Nor days nor things diurnal;
Only the sleep eternal
In an eternal night.

A. C. Swinburne

It is time, heart, to recall,
To recollect, regather all:

The grain is grown,
Reap what was sown
And bring into the barn your corn.

Those fields of childhood, tall
Meadow-grass and flowers small,
The elm whose dusky leaves
Patterned the sky with dreams innumerable
And labyrinthine vein and vine
And wandering tendrils green,
Have grown a seed so small
A single thought contains them all.

The white birds on their tireless wings return,
Spent feather, flesh and bone let fall,
And the blue distances of sea and sky
Close within the closing eye
As everywhere comes nowhere home.
Draw in my heart
Those golden rays whose threads of light
The visible veil of world have woven,
And through the needle's eye
Upon that river bright
Travels the laden sun
Back from its voyage through the night.

We depart and part,
We fail and fall

Till love calls home
All who our separate lonely ways have gone.

Kathleen Raine, from *The Hollow Hill*

ON THE DEATHS OF CHILDREN

THE BURIAL OF AN INFANT

Blest Infant Bud, whose Blossom-life
Did only look about, and fall,
Wearied out in a harmless strife
Of tears, and milk, the food of all;

Sweetly didst thou expire: thy soul
Flew home unstain'd by his new kin,
For ere thou knew'st how to be foul,
Death wean'd thee from the world, and sin.

Softly rest all thy Virgin-crumbs!
Lapt in the sweets of thy young breath,
Expecting till thy Saviour comes,
To dress them, and unswaddle death.

Henry Vaughan

It is not growing like a tree
In bulk doth make man better be;
Or standing long an oak, three hundred year,
To fall a log at last, dry, bald, and sere;
A lily of a day
Is fairer far in May,
Although it fall and die that night,
It was the plant and flower of light.
In small proportions we just beauty see,
And in short measures life may perfect be.

Ben Jonson

ON THE DEATH OF A CHILD

The greatest griefs shall find themselves inside
the smallest cage.
It's only then that we can hope to tame their
rage,

The monsters we must live with. For it will not
do
To hiss humanity because one human threw
Us out of heart and home. Or part

At odds with life because one baby failed to
live.
Indeed, as little as its subject, is the wreath we
give —

The big words fail to fit. Like giant boxes
Round small bodies. Taking up improper room,
Where so much withering is, and so much
   bloom.

D. J. Enright

ON THE DEATH OF A GRANDCHILD

Farewell dear babe, my heart's too much
   content,
Farewell, sweet babe, the pleasure of mine eye,
Farewell fair flower that for a space was lent,
Then ta'en away unto Eternity.
Blest babe, why should I once bewail thy fate,
Or sigh thy days so soon were terminate,
Since thou art settled in an Everlasting state?

Anne Bradstreet
(in memory of Elizabeth Bradstreet who died in
   August 1665, being a year and a half old)

DOOMED TO KNOW NOT WINTER

Doomed to know not Winter, only Spring – a
   being
Trod the flowery April blithely for a while;
Took his fill of music, joy of thought and
   seeing,

Came and stayed and went; nor ever ceased to
smile.

Came and stayed and went; and now, when all
is finished,
You alone have crossed the melancholy stream.
Yours the pang; but his, oh his, the
undiminished
Undecaying gladness, undeparted dream.

R. L. Stevenson

A PRAYER FOR COMFORT

For all who are bearing great pain, and who wonder, like lost and bewildered children, why their
Father does not come to them, if not to deliver, at
least to comfort and be consciously *there* to sustain
them.

For all sufferers for whom the lonely hours pass
so very slowly on leaden feet; who wonder in the
dawn however they will get through the day, and
who, all through the endless night, look at the time
again and again, wondering whether the dark hours
will ever pass. . . .

For all who feel that God has left them to bear
their pain uncomforted and alone, that they may
hold on in the dark without despair, and that SOON
may come peace, and the soothing and unutter-

able comfort of Thy Divine Spirit in their hearts. Amen.

Leslie Weatherhead, *A Private House of Prayer*

SURPRISED BY JOY

Surprised by joy – impatient as the Wind
I turned to share the transport – Oh! with
    whom
But thee, deep buried in the silent tomb,
That spot which no vicissitude can find?
Love, faithful love, recalled thee to my mind –
But how could I forget thee? Through what
    power,
Even for the least division of an hour,
Have I been so beguiled as to be blind
To my most grievous loss! – That thought's
    return
Was the worst pang that sorrow ever bore,
Save one, one only, when I stood forlorn,
Knowing my heart's best treasure was no more;
That neither present time, nor years unborn
Could to my sight that heavenly face restore.

William Wordsworth (on the death of his
    daughter Catharine aged 4)

FOR CHILDREN WHO DIE BEFORE BIRTH

NOT TO BE BORN

No different, I said, from rat's or chicken's,
That ten-week protoplasmic blob. But you
Cried as if you knew all that was nonsense
And knew that I did, too.

Well, I had to say something. And there
Seemed so little anyone could say.
That life had been in women's wombs before
And gone away?

This was our life. And yet, when the dead
Are mourned a little, then become unreal,
How should the never born be long
    remembered?
So this in time will heal

Though now I cannot comfort. As I go
The doctor reassures: 'Straightforward case.
You'll find, of course, it leaves her rather low.'
Something is gone from your face.

David Sutton

A CHILD BORN DEAD

What ceremony can we fit
You into now? If you had come
Out of a warm and noisy room
To this, there'd be an opposite
For us to know you by. We could
Imagine you in lively mood

And then look at the other side,
The mood drawn out of you, the breath
Defeated by the power of death.
But we have never seen you stride
Ambitiously the world we know.
You could not come and yet you go.

But there is nothing now to mar
Your clear refusal of our world.
Not in our memories can we mould
You or distort your character.
Then all our consolation is
That grief can be as pure as this.

Elizabeth Jennings

PRAYER ON THE DEATH OF A CHILD

Almighty God, giver of every good and perfect gift, we thank you for the happiness and love this child has brought and for the assurance we have that she/ he is in your care. Strengthen us to commit ourselves to your gracious providence, so that we may live our lives here in the peace and joy of faith, until at last we are united with all the children of God in the brightness of your glory. Amen.

PRAYER FOR THE LITTLE DAUGHTER BETWEEN DEATH AND BURIAL

Now you are standing face to face with the clear
    light
believe in it
Now you have gone back into where air comes
    from
hold fast to it
Now you have climbed to the top of the topless
    tower
and there are no stairs down
and the only way is flight past the edge of the
    world
do not remember us

Like the new moon in the sky of the shortest
    day
you came to us
as the candles burnt with a steady light behind
    misty windows
you whispered to us
as the singers moved behind doors of
    un-attainable rooms
you burst in on us
Lady of the shortest day, silent upon the
    threshold
carrying green branches

Lady of the crown of light going into clear light
be safe on your journey
Bright lady of the dark day, who pushed back
    the darkness
say nothing to us
as we plod through the frozen field
going somewhere to somewhere
do not speak to us
as we stand at the centre of the frozen lake
and trees of cloud stand over us
forget us

When we come to you we shall find you
who have seen Persephone
you whom our mothers called Lady of the city
will welcome us with tapers, and believe in us

When small harsh birds bubble and pump in
    our nude trees
and water will rush and gush through the
    slipper street
and two skies will look at each other
one of air and one below
of water
you will rest with us, and of us;
Lady of the shortest day
watch over our daughter
whom we commit to the grass.

Diana Scott

ON THE TRANSIENCE OF HUMAN LIFE

In the midst of life we are in death.

Man that is born of a woman hath but a short time
to live and is full of sorrow. He cometh up and is
cut down, like a flower; he fleeth as it were a shadow,
and never continueth in one stay.

We brought nothing into this world and it is certain we can carry nothing out. The Lord gave and
the Lord hath taken away. Yet, O Lord God most
holy, O Lord most mighty, O holy and most merciful
Saviour, deliver us not into the bitter pains of eternal
death.

LAST WORDS

I do not want a plain box, I want a sarcophagus
With tigery stripes, and a face on it
Round as the moon, to stare up.
I want to be looking at them when they come
Picking among the dumb minerals, the roots.
I see them already – the pale, star-distance
    faces.
Now they are nothing, they are not even babies.
I imagine them without fathers or mothers, like
    the first gods.
They will wonder if I was important.
I should sugar and preserve my days like fruit!
My mirror is clouding over –
A few more breaths, and it will reflect nothing
    at all.
The flowers and the faces whiten to a sheet.

I do not trust the spirit. It escapes like steam
In dreams, through mouth-hole or eye-hole. I
    can't stop it.
One day it won't come back. Things aren't like
    that.
They stay, their little particular lustres
Warmed by much handling. They almost purr.
When the soles of my feet grow cold,
The blue eye of my turquoise will comfort me.

Let me have my copper cooking pots, let my
   rouge pots
Bloom about me like night flowers, with a good
   smell.
They will roll me up in bandages, they will
   store my heart
Under my feet in a neat parcel.
I shall hardly know myself. It will be dark,
And the shrine of these small things sweeter
   than
                              the face of Ishtar.

   Sylvia Plath

SONG

When I am dead, my dearest,
   Sing no sad songs for me;
Plant thou no roses at my head,
   Nor shady cypress tree;
Be the green grass above me
   With showers and dewdrops wet;
And if thou wilt, remember,
   And if thou wilt, forget.

I shall not see the shadows,
   I shall not feel the rain;
I shall not hear the nightingale
   Sing on as if in pain,

And dreaming through the twilight
　That doth not rise nor set,
Haply I may remember,
　And haply may forget.

Christina Rossetti

MEDITATION

A late lark twitters from the quiet skies;
And from the west,
Where the sun, his day's work ended,
Lingers as in content,
There falls on the old grey city
An influence luminous and serene,
A shining peace.

The smoke ascends
In a rosy and golden haze. The spires
Shine, and are changed. In the valley
Shadows rise. The lark sings on. The sun,
Closing his benediction,
Sings, and the darkening air
Thrills with a sense of the triumphing night –
Night with her train of stars
And her great gift of sleep.

So be my passing!
My task accomplished and the long day done,

My wages taken, and in my heart
Some late lark singing,
Let me be gathered to the quiet west,
The sundown splendid and serene,
Death.

W. E. Henley

The wise in heart mourn not for those that live, nor those that die. Never the spirit was born; the spirit shall cease to be never. Never was time the spirit was not. End and Beginning are dreams! Death hath not touched it at all, dead though the house of it seems! Nay, as when one layeth his worn-out robes away, and, taking new ones, sayeth, 'These will I wear today!' so putteth by the spirit lightly its garb of flesh, and passeth to inherit a residence afresh.

Bhagavad Gita, II, 19–22

CROSSING THE BAR

Sunset and evening star,
  And one clear call for me!
And may there be no moaning of the bar,
  When I put out to sea,

But such a tide as moving seems asleep,
  Too full for sound and foam,

When that which drew from out the boundless
  deep
  Turns again home.

Twilight and evening bell,
  And after that the dark!
And may there be no sadness of farewell,
  When I embark;

For tho' from out our bourne of Time and Place
  The flood may bear me far,
I hope to see my Pilot face to face
  When I have crossed the bar.

Alfred Lord Tennyson

DIRGE WITHOUT MUSIC

I am not resigned to the shutting away of loving
  hearts in the hard ground.
So it is, and so it will be, for so it has been,
  time out of mind;
Into the darkness they go, the wise and the
  lovely. Crowned
With lilies and with laurel they go; but I am not
  resigned.

Lovers and thinkers, into the earth with you.
Be one with the dull, the indiscriminate dust.

A fragment of what you felt, of what you knew,
A formula, a phrase remains, – but the best is
  lost.

The answers quick and keen, the honest look,
  the laughter, the love –
They are gone. They are gone to feed the roses.
  Elegant and curled
Is the blossom. Fragrant is the blossom. I
  know. But I do not approve.
More precious was the light in your eyes than
  all the roses in the world.

Down, down, down into the darkness of the
  grave
Gently they go, the beautiful, the tender, the
  kind,
Quietly they go, the intelligent, the witty, the
  brave
I know. But I do not approve. And I am not
  resigned.

Edna St Vincent Millay

DO NOT GO GENTLE INTO THAT GOOD NIGHT

Do not go gentle into that good night,
Old age should burn and rave at close of day;
Rage, rage against the dying of the light.

Though wise men at their end know dark is
    right,
Because their words had forked no lightning
    they
Do not go gentle into that good night.

Good men, the last wave by, crying how bright
Their frail deeds might have danced in a green
    bay,
Rage, rage against the dying of the light.

Wild men who caught and sang the sun in
    flight,
And learn, too late, they grieved it on its way,
Do not go gentle into that good night.

Grave men, near death, who see with blinding
    sight
Blind eyes could blaze like meteors and be gay,
Rage, rage against the dying of the light.

And you, my father, there on the sad height,
Curse, bless, me now with your fierce tears, I
    pray.
Do not go gentle into that good night
Rage, rage against the dying of the light.

Dylan Thomas

STOP ALL THE CLOCKS, CUT OFF THE TELEPHONE

Stop all the clocks, cut off the telephone,
Prevent the dog from barking with a juicy bone,
Silence the pianos and with muffled drum
Bring out the coffin, let the mourners come.

Let aeroplanes circle moaning overhead
Scribbling on the sky the message He is Dead,
Put the crepe bows round the white necks of the
    public doves,
Let the traffic policemen wear black cotton
    gloves.

He was my North, my South, my East and
    West,
My working week and my Sunday rest,
My noon, my midnight, my talk, my song;
I thought that love would last for ever; I was
    wrong.

The stars are not wanted now: put out every
    one;
Pack up the moon and dismantle the sun;
Pour away the ocean and sweep up the wood.
For nothing now can ever come to any good.

W. H. Auden

THE COMMITTAL

Forasmuch as it hath pleased Almighty God of his great mercy to take unto himself the soul of our dear brother/sister here departed, we therefore commit his/her body to the ground; earth to earth, ashes to ashes, dust to dust. In certain hope of the Resurrection to eternal life, through our Lord Jesus Christ.

JEWISH FUNERAL PRAYER

In the presence of death let us not fear. We share it with all who have ever lived and with all who will ever be. For it is only the dust which returns to the dust as it was, but the spirit returns to God who gave it, and in His hand is the care of every soul. The world we inhabit is a corridor to the world beyond. We prepare ourselves in the corridor to enter His presence. He is our employer who knows our sorrows and our labour. Faithful is He to give us the reward of our good deeds. He redeems us from destruction and leads us in the way of everlasting life.

ON THE SCATTERING OF ASHES

Then let my ashes be scattered abroad – not collected in an urn – freely sown wide and broadcast. That is the natural interment of man – of man whose thought at least has been among the Immortals; interment in the elements. The high open air of the topmost hill . . . there cast the ashes into the space it longed for while living.

Give me still more, for the interminable universe, past and present, is but earth; give me the unknown soul, the soul of which I know only that when I touch the ground, when the sunlight touches my hand, it is not there. . . . As the sky extends beyond the valley, so I know that there are ideas beyond the valley of my thought. . . . There is an immense ocean over which the mind can sail. . . . There is so much beyond all that has ever yet been imagined.

Richard Jeffries, from *The Story of my Heart*

GOING INTO THE UNKNOWN

There is so much beyond all that has ever yet been imagined. As I write these words, in the very moment, I feel that the whole air, the sunshine out yonder lighting up the ploughed earth, the distant sky, the circum-ambient ether, and that far space, is full of soul-secrets, soul-life, things outside the experience of all the ages. The fact of my own exist- ence, as I exist at this second, is so marvellous, so miracle-like, strange and supernatural to me that I unhesitatingly conclude that I am always on the margin of the life illimitable and that there are higher conditions than existence. Everything around is supernatural; everything so full of unexplained meaning. . . . From earth and sea and sun, from night, the stars, from day, the trees, the hills, from my own soul – I stand this moment . . . face to face with nature, face to face with the supernatural, with myself. My naked mind confronts the unknown.

Richard Jeffries, from *The Story of my Heart*

Lead me from death to life, from falsehood to
truth;
Lead me from despair to hope, from fear to
trust;
Lead me from hate to love, from war to peace;
Let peace fill our hearts,
Our world,
Our universe.

From *The Upanishads*

The power of the moon be with you
The power of the sun be with you
The power of the rain be with you

The power of the sea be with you
The power of land be with you
The power of the stars be with you
The power of heaven be with you
The power of the universe be with you.

A part of you be on the grey stones
A part of you on the steep mountains
A part of you on the swift waterfalls
A part of you on the gleaming clouds
A part of you on the ocean whales
A part of you on the meadow beasts
A part of you on the marshy swamps
A part of you on the bog-cottoned moors
A part of you on the green fields
A part on the great surging ocean
And may the power of the universe be with you.

Adapted from *Carmina Gadelica*

FAREWELL SWEET DUST

Now I have lost you, I must scatter
All of you on the air henceforth;
Not that to me it can ever matter
But it's only fair to the rest of earth.

Now especially, when it is winter
And the sun's not half so bright as he was,

Who wouldn't be glad to find a splinter
That once was you, in the frozen grass?

Snowflakes too, will be softer feathered,
Clouds, perhaps, will be whiter plumed;
Rain, whose brilliance you caught and gathered,
Purer silver have reassumed.

Farewell, sweet dust; I was never a miser:
Once, for a minute, I made you mine:
Now you are gone, I am none the wiser
But the leaves of the willow are bright as wine.

Elinor Wylie

END PAGE

In the night watch over me.
Keep that which would deny life cornered.
Let there be a place at tables for all those that
    mourn.
May earth, sea, and sky
always be remembered, blessed.
May love never have to justify its name.

Clare Crossman

VALEDICTION

I said to the man who stood at the Gate of the
   Year:
'Give me a light, that I may tread safely into
   the unknown.'
And he replied:
'Go out into the darkness and put your hand
   into the hand of God.
That shall be to you better than light and safer
   than a known way.'
So I went forth, and finding the hand of God,
   trod gladly into the night
And He led me toward the hills and the
   breaking of day in the lone East.

Minnie Louise Haskins, *God Knows*

MUSIC

There is a wide variety of live music that can be used to enhance a funeral service. A gospel choir, a Celtic harpist, organist, traditional jazz band, or a lone piper to lead the procession and play over the grave. Your local arts development agency (contact your local council) may be able to help you, or there may be addresses at your local library. If not try the Arts Council or the Musician's Union.

Paying professional musicians can be costly, so you might prefer to use a tape recording or CD of the deceased's favourite music. The suggestions in the following list should be easily available.

CLASSICAL

Albinoni: *Adagio in G minor* for organ and strings
Allegri: *Miserere*
Bach: *Sheep May Safely Graze* (Cantata no. 208)
Barber: *Adagio for Strings*
Beethoven: Adagio from *Symphony no. 9*
Jan Gabarek and The Hilliard Ensemble: *Officium* (saxophone and Gregorian chant)
Handel: 'Eternal source of light divine' from *Ode on the Birthday of Queen Anne*
  'I know that my Redeemer liveth' from *Messiah*
  Largo from *Xerxes*
Mahler: *Kindertotenlieder* (songs on the Deaths of Children)
Marcello: Adagio from *Oboe Concerto in D minor*
Massenet: Meditation from *Thais*
Mozart: *Requiem*
Puccini: 'Nessun dorma' from *Turandot*
Purcell: 'Dido's Lament' from *Dido and Aeneas*
  Solemn March and Canzona from *Music for the Funeral of Queen Mary*
Rodrigo: Adagio from *Concierto de Aranjuez*
Satie: *Trois gnossiennes*
Strauss: *Metamorphosis*
Vaughan Williams: *The Lark Ascending*
  Toward the Unknown Region
Verdi: 'Dies irae' from the *Requiem*
Vivaldi: 'Autumn' or 'Winter' from *Four Seasons*

'Gloria in excelsis Deo' and 'Cum Sancto Spiritu' from *Gloria in D*, RV 589
'In memoria aeterna' from *Beatus vir in C*, RV 597

TRADITIONAL AND POPULAR

Clannadh: Theme from *Harry's Game* (Celtic)
Deep River (American spiritual)
Enya: *Orinoco Flow, Watermark* (Celtic)
Far Corporation: *Stairway to Heaven*
Whitney Houston: *I Will Always Love You*
Elton John: *Candle in the Wind*
Peter King: *Tamburello* (Jazz requiem for Ayrton Senna)
Ladysmith Black Mambazo: selection of Zulu vocal music
Bette Midler and Whitney Houston: *You are the Wind beneath my Wings*
Missa Luba (African Mass)
O'Carolan's Receipt (Celtic harp music based on tunes by Turlough O'Carolan, 1670–1738)
Edith Piaf: *No Regrets*
Righteous Brothers: *Unchained Melody*
Simon and Garfunkel: *Bridge over Troubled Water*
Sky: Selection for meditation (Celtic)
Barbra Streisand: *Memories*
Swing Low, Sweet Chariot
When the Saints come Marching In

USEFUL PUBLICATIONS

Judi Benson, ed., *The Long Pale Corridor: Anthology of Poems on Bereavement*, Bloodaxe, 1996

J. Bentley, A. Best and J. Hunt, ed., *Funerals: A Guide to Prayers, Hymns and Readings*, Hodder & Stoughton, 1994

D. J. Enright, ed., *The Oxford Book of Death*, Oxford University Press, 1987

Funerals Without God, British Humanist Association, 1989 (£5.00 inc p&p)

Sue Gill and John Fox, *The Dead Good Funerals Book*, Welfare State International, 1996

How to Direct your own Funeral: A Practical Handbook, Bookstall Publications, 1992 (available from Independent Funerals Advisory Service: see address list)

Charles Mosley, Debrett's Guide to Bereavement
(Practical guidance for coping with loss of a loved
one), Headline, 1995
The Natural Death Handbook, Natural Death
Centre, 1997 (see address list)
Sogyal Rinpoche, *The Tibetan Book of Living and
Dying*, Random House, 1992
*What to do after a Death in England and Wales/
Scotland*, DHSS
Wiccan Rites, *Crossing the Bridge at Death* (available
from the Pagan Federation: see address list)

USEFUL ADDRESSES

British Buddhist Association, 11 Biddulph Road, London W9 1JA. Tel. 0171 286 5575
British Humanist Association, 47 Theobald's Road, London WC1X 8SP. Tel. 0171 430 0908
Ceramic Ash Containers from Tim Hurn, Home Farm House, Bettiscombe, Bridport, Dorset DT6 5NU
Child Bereavement Trust, Harleyford Estate, Henley Road, Marlow, Bucks S17 2DX. Tel. 01628 48801
Child Death Helpline, Bereavement Services Department, Great Ormond Street Hospital, 40–41 Queen Square, London WC1N 3AJ. Tel. 0800 282986
Compassionate Friends (offer friendship and support for bereaved parents and other adults), 53 North Street, Bristol BS3 1EN. Tel. 01179 539639

The Cremation Society of Great Britain, 2nd Floor Brecon House, 16/16A Albion Place, Maidstone, Kent ME14 5DZ. Tel. 01622 688292

Dragonpaths, 12 Sandbed Road, St Werburghs, Bristol BS2 9TX. Tel. 01179 411557

Engineers of the Imagination, The Ellers, Ulverston, Cumbria LA12 0AA. Tel. 01229 581127

Vic Fearn & Co. Ltd, Coffin Makers (will supply at short notice if required – a range of coffins from simple boxes to more elaborate caskets, including recycled timber and environmentally friendly ones), Crabtree Mill, Hempshill Lane, Bulwell, Nottingham NG6 8PF. Tel. 0115 9771571

Funerals Direct, Ercall House, 6 Whitchurch Road, Wellington, Telford TF1 3AG. Tel. 01952 251125

The Garden of Remembrance, PO Box 39018, Victoria, British Columbia V8V4X8, Canada

P. A. Ginns, Compakta Ltd (Cardboard self-assembly coffins; cardboard coffins also available from funeral shops and independent funeral services in this list; Natural Death Centre will supply details of your local stockist), The Old White Cottage, Desford, Leics LE9 9GS. Tel. 01455 828642

Green Undertakings, 44 Swain Street, Watchet, Somerset TA23 0AG. Tel. 01984 632285. Also at Belmont Funerals, Pillmawr Road, Newport NP6 6WF. Tel. 01633 855350

Heaven on Earth, Kingsley House, Cotham Road South, Kingsdown, Bristol BS6 5TZ. Tel. 01179 421836

E. C. Hodge (MF) Ltd, Coffin Makers (will supply coffins for next day delivery), New Drove, Weasenham Lane, Wisbech, Cambs PE13 2RZ. Tel. 01934 587477

Independent Funerals Advisory Service (IFAS), PO Box 1, Watchet, Somerset TA23 0YY. Tel. Fax 01984 632285

Martha's Funerals (all women funeral service), 44 Swain Street, Watchet, Somerset TA23 0AG. Tel. 01984 632285

Memory Boxes from Despatch Services, Barnardo's Child Care Publications, Paycocke Road, Basildon, Essex SS14 3DR

Musicians' Union, National Office, 60–62 Clapham Road, London SW9 0JJ. Tel. 0171 582 5566

National Association of Funeral Directors, 618 Warwick Road, Solihull, West Midlands B91 1AA. Tel. 0121 711 1343

The Natural Death Centre, 20 Heber Road, London NW2 6AA. Tel. 0181 208 2853 Fax 0181 452 5434

Pagan Federation, BM Box 7097, London SC1N 3XX. Tel. 01691 671066. E-mail>Secretary@Pagan-Fed.demon.co.uk

Peace Burials, St Peters Villas, Ridley Lane, Mawdesley, Ormskirk, Lancs L40 3SX. Tel. 01704 821 900

Regale, Funerals Supermarket, 277 Hoe Street, Walthamstow, London E17 9PT. Tel. 0181 925 2010

Quakers (The Religious Society of Friends),

Friends House, 173–177 Euston Road, London NW1 2BJ. Tel. 0171 663 1000

Registrar General, General Register Office, Smedley Hydro, Trafalgar Road, Berkdale, Southport PR8 2HH. Tel. 0151 471 4200

Society of Allied and Independent Funeral Directors, Crowndale House, 1 Ferdinand Place, London NW1 8EE. Tel. 0171 267 6777

Woven Willow Coffins from Chrysalis, The Willow Weave Co., The Goat Shed, Rowancroft, Kenninghall Road, Banham, Norwich NR16 2HE.

WEB SITES

Information on woodland burial sites, how to obtain carton board coffins and details of inexpensive funerals is available on http://newciv.org/worldtrans/naturaldeath.html. For advice on green, family-organised funerals you can access http://www.newciv.org/GIB/befaft/contents.html.

Creative Endings (Designer Dying and Celebratory Funerals): http://www.newciv.org/GIB/crend/CRETOP.HTML.

The Garden of Remembrance: http://www.-islandnet.com/deathnet/garden.html.

The World Wide Cemetery on the Internet: http://www.io.org/cemetery/.